WIN

WIN

WIN

WIN
WIN
WIN

Organizational Success
through the Power of Agreement

BRIAN D. MOLITOR

Authentic

COLORADO SPRINGS • LONDON • HYDERABAD

Authentic Publishing
We welcome your questions and comments.

USA   1820 Jet Stream Drive, Colorado Springs, CO 80921 www.authenticbooks.com
UK   9 Holdom Avenue, Bletchley, Milton Keynes, Bucks, MK1 1QR
        www.authenticmedia.co.uk
India   Logos Bhavan, Medchal Road, Jeedimetla Village, Secunderabad 500 055, A.P.

Win Win Win
ISBN-13: 978-1-934068-05-2
ISBN-10: 1-934068-05-5

Copyright © 2007 by Brian D. Molitor

10 09 08 07 / 6 5 4 3 2 1

Published in 2007 by Authentic
Cover design: Paul Lewis
Interior design: Angela Lewis
Editorial team: Andy Sloan, Megan Kassebaum

Printed in the United States of America

Dedication

This book is dedicated to all who seek to make positive change in the world around them . . .

To the VISIONARIES: As with any great artist, you see what others cannot see. You dream, while others only worry. You act when others only talk. Your gift is frequently misunderstood. Your words are often misquoted, twisted, and mocked. Yet . . . still, you dream. Without your light, our world would be a very dark place. May God inspire you and enlighten you.

To the LEADERS: You harness the power of hearts, minds, and wills to accomplish great things. Your words and actions model excellence for others. Your plans unify purpose. With a wave of your hand, you turn solos into symphonies. Without you, there would be no teams, no teamwork, and no great accomplishments. May God encourage you and refresh you.

To the PEACEMAKERS: You offer hope to nations, cities, companies, homes, and individual hearts. Your gentle wisdom tears down barriers and builds bridges in their place. You boldly stand between warring factions, offering hope of reconciliation. Your gentle words turn anger into reason. Without you our world would be destroyed, one life at a time. May God strengthen you and grant you peace.

Contents

Part 4. Developing the Human Side of the Organizational Equation

Part 5. Keeping the Dream Alive

Acknowledgments

Thanks to all who have been part of my work life over the years . . .

First, to my wife, Kathleen: Thanks for your love and the grace to put up with international travel, publication deadlines, and long hours. Without you, my story would have ended long ago.

To my children, Christopher, Steven, Jenifer, and Daniel: Thanks for sharing your dad with others and for making life such a wonderful adventure. So much of what I have done was for you.

To my parents, Bob and Jinny Molitor: Thanks for the great start and for your support along the way. You both mean the world to me, and I am so glad that you decided to stick around to see how this all turns out.

To my associates and special friends: There have been so many great people in my life over the years. On the short list are Rick Suitor, Harry Marcus, James Glenn, Ron Ferguson, Mark Holmes, Jan Clarkson, Drew Forester, Aaron Glenn, Scotty Hales, Karen Spickerman, Paul Armstrong, Burnett Kelly, Warrick Marsh, Ron and Carla Ives, Geoffrey Stokes, Gene Pickelman, John and Ann Bennett, Rhonda Schiortino, Ric Olson, Joe Affholter, Lanny Robbins, Trevor Knoeson, Brian Pruitt, Ron Williams, Scott McTiernan, Gem Fletcher, and Ontay Johnson.

What a joy to work with those who catch the vision and have the courage to pursue it. Thank you all!

Win/Win . . . Win

The world we live in measures success in terms of winning and losing. In fact, we obsess over the concept of winning. Each morning we turn on the television to see who *won* the game, who *won* the election, or who *won* the latest million-dollar lottery.

Quick video clips of the winners speak volumes about the joys of victory: elation, satisfaction, affirmation, lifelong dreams accomplished. These fine folks will soon be on Oprah, telling the story behind the story. Fame, fortune, and fans are on the way. Why? Because they *won*.

Predictably, those who lost quickly fade and go back to whatever they did before that fateful day. Some never recover from defeat, but instead are consumed by anger, bitterness, whining, or a desire for revenge. The losers' remaining days are often haunted by endless echoes of *what ifs*—just because they lost.

This win/lose, competitive approach to life makes sense for those engaged in sporting events, political races, and pie-eating contests. In such cases there can be only one winner; so, by design, everyone else loses. Those who sign up to compete understand the rules and must live with the final outcome—win or lose.

Healthy competition is certainly not a bad thing. When the win/lose mindset leaches into other realms of life, however, it becomes divisive and destructive. For example, members of the same organization competing against each other sets up a win/lose scenario that signals trouble ahead. Many individuals, fortunately, have learned to replace the traditional win/lose mindset with one that seeks win/win outcomes. That is certainly progress. But we don't have to stop there.

There are many opportunities in this world of business, health care, education, government, ministry, and more for those involved not only to seek win/win outcomes but to go one step further: to win/win . . . win. How is this possible? Here are just a couple of examples.

When managers and employees agree to work together they create a win/win situation. This generates goodwill, increased communication, greater productivity, and so on. These positives spill over and are "caught" by others. Coworkers have a positive model of relationship to follow. Morale increases. Customers receive better products or service. Job security increases. Win/win/win.

In the family setting, a husband and wife stop arguing, declare a truce, and begin working together on their problems. They stop blaming each other and start cooperating, thereby creating a win/win for themselves. The benefits certainly don't stop there. The couple's children, accustomed to living in a war zone, discover that life can be fun. Their sense of well-being increases, as does their focus at school. Report cards are now a source of celebration instead of angry lectures. Win/win/win.

Throughout the world, good organizations have learned to seek win/win outcomes. Those that don't will soon go the way of the dinosaurs and dodo birds. Extinction is assured. It's just a matter of time. Lose/lose . . . lose. However, in the near future the great organizations will be those that go one step further. Win/win/win. This book is written to show you how to make that happen.

PART ONE

Laying the Foundation for Success

CHAPTER 1

Success by Design, or Failure by Default

```
CAUTION:
If you feel pain, faint, or dizzy,
stop immediately.
```

These intimidating words are written on top of the treadmill in my office. They subtly challenge my decision to get in better physical shape each time I step onto the machine. Often, midway through the workout, that one word, *stop,* leaps out at me, and I once again must decide if the future gain is worth the present pain.

This is true in virtually all areas of our personal and professional lives. Despite the fact that change is often difficult, even painful, people throughout the world recognize that they have two fundamental choices when it comes to the future: either boldly set a course for positive change or react to someone else's agenda. Those who believe in the myth of the status quo are only fooling themselves. In fact, the only thing certain about the future is constant change.

Our world regularly experiences change in the realms of politics, religion, trade, ethics, and a host of others. The international marketplace is a hotbed of change, as borders blur and monetary values bob up and down in a sea of uncertainty. Advances in technology transform today's best-selling product into tomorrow's reject. (Have you played any eight-track tapes lately?)

> THE ONLY THING CERTAIN ABOUT THE FUTURE IS CONSTANT CHANGE.

As the waves of unprecedented change in our world continue to roll, we struggle to find ways to cope. Some try to insulate and isolate themselves from the ever-rising tide, quietly comforted by the mantra "This too shall pass." Others attempt to ignore or avoid change. Still others struggle to resist or even sabotage it. None of these strategies ever leads to successful change management.

Fortunately, there is a unique group emerging with the courage and wisdom not only to manage change but also to initiate it. They possess an uncanny ability to perceive things as they should be rather than as they are. Unfazed by the accelerating pace of change, they devise innovative strategies that enable their communities, organizations, and families to prosper. These innovators live much like professional racecar legend Mario Andretti who once said, "If everything seems under control, you're not going fast enough."

Some of these change masters are formal leaders with impressive titles, such as president, chief executive officer, prime minister, senator, or general manager. Others, lacking position or traditional power, are changing their world with rock-solid character and unwavering faith. Positive change is often

> CHANGE AGENTS PERCEIVE THINGS AS THEY SHOULD BE—NOT AS THEY ARE.

borne more of will than skill. It also takes great perseverance. India's champion for civil rights, Mahatma Gandhi, described the process of changing the hearts and minds of others in this way: "First they ignore you, then they laugh at you, then they fight you, then you win."

Regardless of the approach utilized, few individuals have the power to create and sustain a positive change effort alone. In fact, virtually every significant change in society, politics, business, and/or religion begins with a simple four-step process. First,

> EVERY SIGNIFICANT CHANGE IN SOCIETY, POLITICS, BUSINESS, OR RELIGION BEGINS WITH A SIMPLE FOUR-STEP PROCESS.

one or more individuals *realize* that it is time for a change by recognizing that a problem, threat, or opportunity exists. Next, the leader(s) *create* a new vision for the future of their nation, community, organization, family, or personal lives. After that, the leaders *communicate* the vision to others, who then agree to help implement the change. Finally, leaders and followers bond to form effective teams that *commit* to a strategic plan of action, resulting in successful change.

The Secret Ingredient in Successful Change

While historians tell countless stories of dynamic leaders who changed the world for the better, a key ingredient in their success is often overlooked. That ingredient is *agreement*. Gandhi; British statesman Sir Winston Churchill; King David of ancient Israel; American president Abraham Lincoln; Microsoft founder, Bill Gates; civil rights champion Martin Luther King Jr.; and Jesus Christ of Nazareth were leaders who understood the power found only in agreement. In each case, these individual leaders built teams of committed followers whose hard work transformed the vision into reality.

Predictably, these world changers have much in common. Each was an effective communicator who understood that it took many people working together to bring about positive change. In addition, each realized the importance of unleashing the dynamic, self-generating power of a team of people who have agreed upon a course of action. Each of these victors, at one time or another, heard the cheers of the adoring crowd. However, there can be no victory without a war. Therefore each of them clearly experienced suffering, opposition, and what seemed like defeat along the way. They must have had the word *stop* leap out at them during times of severe trial. Yet, rather than give in to the pressures, they courageously stayed on course and blazed a trail for others to follow.

> CHANGE AGENTS SEE WHAT OTHERS FAIL TO SEE AND DO WHAT OTHERS FEAR TO DO.

Some people today view these change agents as heroes, while others disagree with their visions. But all must accept the fact that they made a difference during their brief stay on Planet Earth. They saw what others failed to see; they did what others feared to do.

The Power of Agreement

There are many sources of energy in the world today, including wood, coal, wind, gasoline, nuclear generators, and the sun. Each has some unusual qualities. Only one type of power, however, is truly unique: the power of the human spirit.

While all change agents have tremendous value in and of themselves, a close inspection reveals that the overwhelming number of these transformational miracles were and are the result of multiple people working together. Therein lies the foundation of the dynamic, self-generating power of agreement. It begins with two or more people who agree upon a vision or course of action. Then those people work cooperatively by sharing ideas, motivating each other, jointly solving problems, and implementing strategies to accomplish the vision.

In most instances, two or more people generate results far superior to those they produce working alone. How is this multiplication effect possible? The old saying "Two heads are better than one" helps us to understand the concept, but there is more to it than that.

When faced with a new problem or opportunity to address, an individual draws upon his or her education, training, and experiences to find the path forward. This approach is often sufficient. When a problem is more complex or the opportunity is in a completely new area, that same individual will likely find himself or herself unable to handle the situation. However, if the individual is fortunate enough to be in relationship with others who are willing to work cooperatively, then the odds are good that some innovative approaches will surface through their teamwork, joint analysis, and brainstorming.

> TWO OR MORE PEOPLE GENERATE RESULTS FAR SUPERIOR TO THOSE THEY PRODUCE WORKING ALONE.

Under the proper circumstances, this meeting of the minds actually happens on a deeper level: the level of the heart. In reality, two heads and two *hearts* are better than one. This simply means that when those involved are mentally and emotionally committed to success, they work sacrificially to overcome any challenge, solve any problem, and seize any opportunity. Organizations that harness this power of agreement will achieve superior results, because they understand the value of their people and how to unleash their potential.

The Corporate Culture in Your Organization

The famous sculptor Michelangelo was once asked how he created such beautiful sculptures out of shapeless blocks of granite. He humbly replied that the beauty was always hidden within the stone—he simply removed the parts that hid the beauty.

I am convinced that we each have a similar opportunity when confronted with today's world that often seems so disjointed and ugly. Here's why: In reality, our lives are lived within the context of multiple "organizations," starting with our family, workplace, community, and place of worship—and then, ultimately, in our nation and world. Each organization is comprised of people interacting with each other for a multitude of reasons. In addition, each has a corporate or shared culture. In simplest terms, all corporate cultures consist of three fundamental components: vision, values, and relationships, each of which develops either by design or by default.

Herein lies our opportunity. You see, unless careful attention is continually given to the culture, the vision becomes muddled, the values are compromised, and the relationships break down for a myriad of reasons. When this happens, we can either throw up our hands in surrender or we can roll up our sleeves and rebuild the foundations of the organization. Like Michelangelo, we can discover the true beauty lying dormant there, and then work diligently to remove whatever prevents others from seeing it as well.

Today we desperately need leaders, from all walks of life, to serve as champions of change in business, industry, government, education, health care, and other realms of life. We need people—like you—to create a new vision, to display rock-solid values, and to forge a team ready to release the power necessary for making positive change a reality. That is the power of agreement. That is win/win/win.

Your Greatest Asset

What do the Great Wall of China, Hoover Dam, and the Egyptian pyramids have in common? Just this: each of these massive construction marvels began with a solid foundation. Had they not, they would never have withstood the test of time.

Organizational success is much the same. It begins with a compelling vision; however, it cannot last unless it is built upon an unshakable foundation. In this case, the base material is neither bricks nor cement. Instead, the foundation for building a strong corporate culture is the simple truth that *people are your greatest asset*. Failure to embrace and act upon this truth hinders organizational success in the short term and eventually leads to organization collapse.

Resources, Assets, or Disposable Parts?

The following chapters provide a blueprint for building organizational success. This blueprint only works, however, if the leaders involved begin the building process by laying the proper foundation in regard to the human side of the equation. There are really only two fundamental positions regarding how important, or unimportant, people are to an organization's success.

The first position is that all human beings are created with intrinsic value, so therefore, given the correct environment, they will naturally make immeasurable contributions to an organization's success. These organizations are characterized by empowerment, trust, honest communication, service, and support for people at all levels. Their leaders exist to serve, support, and motivate and to ensure that the people have what they need to fulfill the overall vision. In these environments, the incredible power of agreement is unleashed.

The second position—diametrically opposed to the first—is that people are simply components, much like machines or computers, that the organization needs in order to function. At the extreme, people are viewed as simply disposable parts of the organizational processes, to be discarded whenever convenient. In these organizations, leaders see people as being essentially faceless and nameless, without any real value other than that which they produce when serving the organization's needs. Rarely will leaders of such organizations admit to having such a negative view; their corporate cultures, however, leave little doubt that this is the case.

Endless rules and regulations, tight controls, mistrust, and the lack of empowerment typify such negative environments. Leaders exist to make sure that people do what they are told and to correct those who fail to measure up. In organizations in which people are not trusted, not valued, and not listened to, the only hope is to increase directives, documentation, and intimidation so that—somehow—the *leaders* can get the job done.

While there is certainly middle ground between these two positions, most organizations can be classified in one or the other extreme. The impact of this philosophical difference on an organization's ability to succeed cannot be overstated.

Your Greatest Asset

Robots, kiosks, and computers will never replace the need for people to be integrally involved in organizational life. Why? Because these electronic gadgets can't think, feel, or react to the needs of other human beings. They can't respond to an unusual situation, nor can they innovate when needed. Anyone who has ever known the frustration of calling a "customer service" phone line, only to be sent on an endless loop of transfers by some mindless machine, knows the value of speaking to a real person about real problems.

I am convinced that the most appropriate term for describing people in the organizational setting is *asset,* not *resource.* Here is why. According to the Oxford American College Dictionary, a *resource* is "a stock or supply of money, materials, or staff that can be drawn upon by a person or organization in order to function effectively." An *asset*, however, is defined as "a useful or valuable thing, person, or quality."

This differentiation is important in today's world, in which so many organizations swap their people for machines. Airline ticket agents are replaced by mindless kiosks, telephone operators are dismissed to make room for annoying answering machines, and the list goes on. People are treated simply as resources: something to be drawn upon in order for the organization to function, something to be wholly discarded in favor of new technology whenever possible. This mindset is a mistake and will ultimately lead to marginalized performance for two fundamental reasons.

Reason number 1. Human beings have been divinely equipped to invent, to innovate, and to overcome seemingly insurmountable obstacles. Unlike animals that must move, adapt, or die when faced with life-threatening conditions in their environment, humans literally change the environment itself. Consider all of the amazing discoveries and successes of the past few centuries. Accomplishments in health care, science, space exploration, agriculture, information technology, and a host of other areas demonstrate the wonderful creative power latent within us.

New technology has certainly aided our ability to progress. However, industrial robots, computers, and the avalanche of technological advances today are simply tools with which human beings successfully manage change. Such tools, by themselves, are incapable of making the world a better place. That job has been reserved for those who made the tools in the first place.

Reason number 2. Employees reflect what they see in their leaders. Employees treated with respect will most likely respond with respect and dedication to the organization, employees treated with fairness will most likely respond with fairness and commitment, and so on. However, if a leader causes his or her employees to feel disrespected or devalued, then the response will surely be negative and will impact the employees' work performance.

What is the application of this in today's competitive world? Just this: People are the keys to success in virtually every organization on the face of the earth. The challenge is to have them ready, willing, and able to do whatever it takes for the organization to prosper. Fundamentally, their state of readiness hinges upon their leaders' answer to one simple question: *Are people our most valuable asset?* The answer to that question will shape the organization's philosophy, policies, and principles of operation. It will determine whether proper investments are made in employee education, training, and development. This one critical issue will largely determine the level of an organization's ultimate success.

CHAPTER 3

The Universal Quest for Success

The universal quest for organizational success begins with a statement that at first glance may seem too simple to be of any real use: *All organizations exist for a purpose.* Specifically, they were formed either to create products, provide services, or share information—or, in some instances, to fulfill two or even all three purposes. Therefore, each organization can have definable measures of success. Once these indicators are identified, then the members of the organization can find ways to improve in these areas, thereby achieving greater levels of success. However, if success indicators are not identified, then organizational improvements are very difficult to achieve.

Old Question – New Answers

Today's quest for success is nothing new. In fact, a quarter century ago Thomas J. Peters' book *In Search of Excellence* generated tremendous interest in corporate success and the mysterious concept of "excellence." The book told the stories of organizations that produced superior results in various bottom-line categories. It was released during a period when business and industry in many parts of the world wrestled with increased competition, acknowledging that if they failed to meet their customers' needs, then someone else gladly would.

Spurred on by a combination of personal commitment, national pride, and some good old-fashioned fear, leaders everywhere began talking about excellence and looking for ways to improve their organizations. This introspection spawned significant improvements in a wide variety of organizations, beginning first in manufacturing and then spilling over into education, health care, government, and others. Employees at all levels accepted the fact that they had to satisfy customers who were no longer shy about demanding high-quality service. The once leisurely jog for excellence quickly turned into a match race joined by thousands of hopefuls. Predictably, not everyone would reach the finish line.

> ALL ORGANIZATIONS EXIST EITHER TO CREATE PRODUCTS, PROVIDE SERVICES, OR SHARE INFORMATION.

World-Class Toilet Paper?

The quest for excellence changed not only the focus of leaders but also their vocabularies, as terms such as *world-class* found their way into the mission statements and marketing campaigns of thousands of organizations. Unfortunately, companies with substandard products and services were quick to claim world-class status as well. Over the years, I have sipped what was proclaimed to be world-class coffee, ridden in world-class rental cars, and even encountered world-class industrial toilet paper. I can assure you, however, that none of these products performed in a manner worthy of the title.

Success. This marvelous concept is something that everyone wants, even though few ever feel that they have achieved it. The reason for this paradox is simple. Success is a broad term that describes an extended journey rather than a single destination. Viewed from this perspective, we can more readily measure our progress by identifying multiple mile markers along the way. No rational leader would ever declare his or her business, ministry, or family successful without being able to identify numerous areas of accomplishment. Did the business generate sufficient profit for growth and expansion? Did the restaurant increase sales? Did the ministry reach more people with a life-changing message of hope? Were family relationships strengthened? Any of these results would be cause for celebration and great indicators of success.

Success Indicators

Over the years, I worked with many organizations to subdivide the broad concept of success or excellence into components that are easy to understand and, in most cases, to measure. This practice permits each member of the organization to understand how his or her individual performance contributes to the organization's overall success. It also prevents the sometimes fatal flaw of focusing on an isolated accomplishment in one part of the organization while overlooking a significant problem in another part. For example, a company that increases its production by 10 percent while simultaneously raising its scrap rate by 50 percent has little to cheer about. Success is a very comprehensive concept that requires a systematic process to achieve. The following is a list of success indicators that have application to virtually all organizations today.

1. *Customer Service*

All organizations exist for a purpose, and at least part of that purpose is to satisfy some sort of customer, end user, or recipient of the organization's outputs. A simple definition of *customer* is someone who buys goods or services from another. Many organizations, however, have wisely expanded this definition into more relational terms. Consequently, sales become the natural result of identifying and meeting the needs of others rather than the result of slick or manipulative marketplace strategies.

As simple as it sounds, the best way to understand this success indicator is to combine the term *customer* with the notion of *service*. Blended together, this concept of *customer service* forms the basis for understanding and the bias for action on the part of all members of an organization. The root word, *serve*, provides a very powerful picture of what is required to excel in this arena. We have all had negative experiences of customer *dis*service with waiters, sales representatives, and others who viewed us as folks to be fleeced rather than as unique individuals worthy of caring, professional services.

> CUSTOMERS ARE VIEWED EITHER AS A SOURCE OF REVENUE OR AS AN EXTENSION OF THE ORGANIZATION ITSELF.

While there may be minor variations, there are essentially only two basic paradigms when it comes to customer service. In the first paradigm, customers are viewed solely as a source of revenue or gain. With this mindset, vendors do whatever it takes to get the customer to buy the particular product, service, or ideology they are selling. To summarize this twisted but all too common view, the customer exists to meet the needs of the vendor or service provider.

The second paradigm sees customers as valuable, extended members of the organization itself. In this light, customers exist to be understood, listened to, and provided with honest information, quality goods, and superior service. Revenue from sales and other rewards are the natural results of high-quality customer service. In other words, the vendor or service provider exists to understand the customer and then to meet or exceed his or her needs and expectations.

The gulf between these two mindsets is immeasurable; and in today's world the only type of organization that can survive with a self-centered worldview is one that has virtually no competitors. When you are the only game in town, people have to play. But when customers have options, they will always go where their needs are met *and* where they are treated with respect by those who provide the goods or services.

2. *Quality of Goods and Services*

Quality improvement, like customer service, is a vital component of every organization. As with all success indicators, each organization's products and/or services can be evaluated in terms of overall quality. In addition to products and services, its very methods of operation can also be analyzed for improvement opportunities. For example, school districts interested in quality improvement can measure test scores of its graduating seniors and then discover ways to raise future performance. Government officials can develop a quality index for a variety of important issues, such as crime, infant survival rate, poverty, new business start-ups, and so on.

Once quality has been defined and baseline measurements have been taken, then a strategy can be devised and implemented to improve the performance of each area. The bottom line on the topic of quality improvement is simple: any organization that fails to measure, evaluate, and improve its product and/or service quality will soon be overtaken by the competition.

3. *Productivity*

Productivity and quality have a unique relationship. While quality improvement seeks to make something better, productivity improvement seeks to make something faster, in larger quantities, cheaper, and/or with fewer resources. There are many different approaches to productivity improvement today. They include productivity incentive programs that compensate people based upon their output, the now famous "downsizing," lean manufacturing, time/motion studies, and a host of others.

Regardless of the approach, organizations that achieve the greatest gains in productivity are those that obtain input from people at all levels. In the corporate world, this input is often obtained during informal meetings or during employee surveys. Input can also be given in formal structures, such as employee empowerment programs, employee involvement teams, natural work groups, and quality improvement teams. In virtually every organization on earth, input from those involved in the production of goods or in customer service is extremely beneficial.

Many leaders have learned that the people closest to a task are the experts, and their input should be used when analyzing options for productivity improvement. Over the years, I have worked with countless productivity improvement efforts, and I am always impressed by the productivity-related innovations discovered by well-trained teams. Productivity skyrockets when employees are given opportunities to study and recommend changes to workflow redesign, new raw material requirements, work assignments, operations layout, and other critical aspects of the operation.

> THE PEOPLE CLOSEST TO THE TASK ARE THE EXPERTS.

4. Waste Reduction

The worldwide concern for protecting and restoring the environment has focused attention on the broad topic of waste reduction. This ranges from toxic waste storage to recycling junk mail. Organizations interested in making positive change in this area also must challenge their institutional enemies of status quo and precedent. Gone are the days when unscrupulous individuals polluted the earth without consequences. Gone too are the wasteful practices of throwing out recyclable materials or allowing careless manufacturing practices to continue unchecked—at least in successful companies.

I recall an amazing example of this that occurred in a candle making company in the Midwestern United States. During a plant tour I stopped to watch a kindly woman who served as the final inspector for one particular line of candles. On either side of her were boxes into which she placed the candles after a quick inspection. After several minutes I observed that the box on her left filled rapidly while the box on her right remained nearly empty. The ratio seemed to be about twenty to one. Impressed with her ability to spot good quality and the obvious efficiency with which the plant operated, I complimented her on the overflowing box of "good" candles. Without taking her eyes off of her machine, she laughed and explained that the full box contained the rejects, and what I thought was scrap were actually the products that made it through inspection. Shocked, I asked what she did with the rejects. She matter-of-factly explained that twice each hour another employee simply came by, picked up the box, and then unceremoniously dumped the rejects back into a vat to be melted down for another try. When I asked how long that practice had been tolerated, the middle-aged woman smiled again and said, "As long as I have been here."

5. *Growth Rate*

Wise leaders in business, ministry, government, health care, and other organizations constantly watch for growth opportunities. They explore the impact of enlarging existing facilities, adding new product lines, expanding services, and/or diversifying. Of course, any expansion must be managed carefully to prevent destabilizing existing operations and/or causing the organization to compromise quality, profitability, or customer service. Failure to do so causes the growth to actually harm the organization rather than help it.

One of our small corporate clients barely survived a bout of unmanaged growth several years ago. They launched a new product that really took off in the marketplace. Soon their workforce ballooned to over six hundred employees as the new product resulted in unprecedented—and unplanned for—demand. The downside of the growth was that the organization had nowhere to put all of the new people. Makeshift desks and work stations sprang up like mushrooms after a spring rain. The communication system was inadequate and soon customer calls were routed throughout the growing office complex in vain attempts to locate the proper people. Predictably, many of the new customers grew so frustrated by the poor service and terrible communications that they went elsewhere. The management of that company focused so intently on whether it *could* continue to grow that it failed to consider whether it *should* continue to grow.

Of course, many organizations today have become stagnant and would gladly sell their corporate souls for a few years of 20 percent growth. A healthy organization must always watch for ways to expand, but it must likewise always weigh the decision carefully before leaping ahead. Careful planning will eliminate all but the most hidden causes of organizational failure. The proper balance here is achieved by walking the path toward healthy growth while avoiding the pitfalls associated with stagnation or destructive expansion.

6. Employment Security and Organizational Loyalty

These two issues have always been related. In today's unpredictable world, however, they are inseparable. In the past people often went to work for a company and then, a quarter century later, retired from that same organization. The gold watch and pension were mainstays of the workplace in the past. This is hardly true today.

In this topsy-turvy marketplace, many organizations are "downsizing," which is today's sanitized term for dismissing employees. In many parts of the world the constant threat of layoffs has created a universal uneasiness within the ranks of white-collar and blue-collar employees alike. This lack of certainty creates huge problems for everyone involved. Companies find it difficult to plan more than a few months ahead, and employees find it hard to concentrate on the work at hand. The result of this lack of employment security? The best and brightest employees often jump ship before they lose their jobs to layoffs. In addition, the performance of those who remain often plummets

> LEADERS WHO ARE CONCERNED WITH EMPLOYEE WELL-BEING ARE REWARDED WITH EXCELLENT COOPERATION AND PRODUCTIVITY, EVEN DURING TOUGH TIMES.

as their loyalty to the organization dwindles. Despite the trend, it does not have to be this way. In fact, leaders who are legitimately concerned about their followers' security and well-being are rewarded with excellent cooperation and productivity, even during the toughest times.

7. Cost Containment and Profitability

A wonderful old song tells us that "love makes the world go 'round." While that may be true, it takes money to do most everything else. Virtually every organization on earth needs some sort of revenue in order to function. Churches, businesses, hospitals, and families all require a certain level of funding to operate or they will struggle for survival.

Once an organization is up and running, it has two essential methods to better itself financially. It can contain and lower its costs, or it can increase its revenues. Profit is not a dirty word, and no organization should ever apologize for making profits from its operations. In fact, this is one of the most common and legitimate measures of organizational success.

8. Organizational Longevity

Organizational success is like a person's honor. It can only be truly evaluated over an extended period. Just as in a football game, it is impossible to determine the winner until the end. One team may have a commanding lead early in the contest, only to lose to a more determined opponent in the final seconds.

The business world needs to revolutionize its thinking if it is ever going to reach and sustain its maximum potential. We must begin to measure progress in years rather than in ninety-day "quarters" as many organizations currently do. This short-term thinking creates tremendous pressure on managers to pursue short-term results—often at the expense of long-term goals—just to appease stockholders or overly demanding executives. Equipment is often operated too long without repair. Employees and their supervisors are worked to the point of exhaustion as product quality slips. These practices lead to anything but excellence. True and lasting excellence is achieved when we plan, reward performance, create supplier and customer alliances, and reinvest in our organizations on a long-term basis.

> JUST AS IN A FOOTBALL GAME, IT IS IMPOSSIBLE TO DETERMINE ORGANIZATIONAL SUCCESS UNTIL THE END.

9. Relationships – Internal and External

Top leaders today understand that long-term success comes from having productive relationships with all of the people involved with the organization. Internally, this includes customers, suppliers, managers, supervisors, employees, stockholders, and volunteers. Externally, it widens to include employees' families, civic leaders, representatives of the press, neighbors, and other members of the community in which the organization is located.

Many organizations have learned the hard way that if they fail to build and maintain productive, trust-based relationships their long-tern success is jeopardized. For example, companies whose leaders work well with suppliers and customers but have poor relationships with their own employees invariably find productivity and/or quality declining. Other companies whose leaders work well with employees but fail to build cooperative relationships with customers may have a wonderful work environment, but they soon may be out of business. This foundational principle holds true in all types of organizations, including churches, governments, education, and health care.

Without question, the lack of focus on relationships is the number one limiting factor—and, potentially, the fatal flaw—in countless organizations around the world today. This is far more than a hunch. It is supported by the testimonies of thousands of employees, supervisors, and managers. During business and ministry training seminars, my staff often asks those in attendance to estimate the level of productivity that their organization is currently achieving. Amazingly, their responses range from 30 to 50 percent. In other words, the amount

> LONG-TERM SUCCESS COMES FROM HAVING PRODUCTIVE RELATIONSHIPS WITH EVERYONE INVOLVED, INCLUDING EMPLOYEES, CUSTOMERS, AND SUPPLIERS.

of work, productivity, quality, cost savings, and profitability that is lost ranges from 50 to 70 percent!

With neither pride nor shame, the people then explain that these horrific numbers come from just one primary source: poor interpersonal relationships within their organization. The lack of focus on relationships invariably squelches communication, kills innovation, and forces people to invent their own self-centered goals and priorities. In these sad settings, work slows, quality falls, and soon new policies are instituted to force, rather than motivate, people to do their jobs. Predictably, employee policy manuals and rule books expand, punishments stiffen, factions develop, and vital relationships get pushed farther apart.

The Bottom Line on Success

Our world is filled with businesses, governments, ministries, and families that are struggling despite having all of the resources they need to succeed. Why? Because they fail to realize that their success depends on how effectively they manage essential relationships. Further, success comes when people build the high-quality relationships necessary to come into agreement about their organization's mission, goals, and values. Simply put, this is what the power of agreement is all about. Without it, no organization will ever achieve and maintain optimum levels of success.

In summary, success must be measured over time by evaluating multiple indicators. In the broadest sense, organizational success occurs when a group of individuals discover, pursue, and accomplish the purpose for which they have been created—and they do so in a manner consistent with their values. Is this really possible? Yes. There are a few road blocks, however, that must be overcome along the way.

> OUR WORLD IS FILLED WITH ORGANIZATIONS THAT STRUGGLE DESPITE HAVING ALL THE RESOURCES THEY NEED TO SUCCEED.

CHAPTER 4

Road Blocks to Success

I have good news and bad news. The bad news is that every effort to create a positive corporate culture will be challenged. The good news is that most of those challenges are predictable and, once identified, can be overcome.

Here are some of the most common challenges faced by leaders attempting to make improvements in organizations of all types, whether nations, businesses, schools, ministries, or families.

Challenge #1: Resistance to Change

Mark Twain once said that the only person who likes change is a baby with a wet diaper. As for the rest of us, we get comfortable with life's routines and resist any change in our personal world. This tendency is so strongly entrenched that we often tolerate a bad situation rather than risk something new. Why? Because every significant change brings with it many unknowns, and fear of the unknown often has a paralyzing effect on the human will. Examples of this are all around us. People work at jobs that barely supply enough income to meet their needs because they fear leaving the security of the known. As bizarre as it seems, some women stay married to abusive husbands for the same reason; predictable misery seems better than the uncertainties of change. This same mindset exists in the business world, where managers and employees alike recognize that their company is on a collision course with disaster and yet they fail to make the changes needed to survive.

Just remember that despite the fact that resistance to change is universal, it can be overcome with a strategic plan and a great deal of hard work. For now, it is important to realize that regardless of what changes you need to make within your organization, the odds are very good that your efforts will be resisted by others until they understand the ultimate vision and how it will benefit their own lives.

Challenge #2: Lack of Trust

Positive change efforts are often hindered by a lack of trust. Employees ignore warnings of economic disaster by corporate officers. Why? Because they have heard the same words during times of prosperity and simply fail to believe that a real threat exists. Politicians who make promises to their constituents and then fail to keep them are soon handicapped in their pursuit of progress for the same reason. Credibility is lost, commitment drops, and people shift back into a "wait and see" mode of operation until trust is rebuilt. The reason is simple. Once bitten, twice shy. Broken trust, at any level, takes time to rebuild.

Challenge #3: Past Failures

"We tried that before and it didn't work." This statement is often heard when someone suggests a change of any kind. Whether it involves empowering corporate employees or reconciling a broken relationship, someone will whine these infamous words. What these doubters overlook is that, although the statement may be true, it fails to recognize one of the greatest qualities of the human race: we have an innate ability to learn, grow, and change.

Today we can analyze yesterday's defeats and turn them into

tomorrow's victories. The husband who sincerely desires to make his marriage work after several failed attempts will probably succeed. Why? Because he has experienced the pain of loneliness and his broken heart demands another try. He has checked his priorities and sees value in the family that he once ignored. He has sought wise counselors, read books on the subject of marriage, and learned to manage his time, money, and other resources in order to accomplish his goals. He has changed. Personal pain is an unpleasant teacher, but an effective one.

The same principle holds true for a company, church, or government that has stumbled in the past but is now committed to making positive change. They can learn. They can grow. They can change.

We desperately need to free ourselves from the shackles of past mistakes and failed attempts if we are going to succeed in changing our world. In one sense, we need to become like children again, in order to rekindle the wonderful quality of faith in things that we cannot see. It is not as hard as it sounds. In fact, we have done it for years. As children, the first time we tried to walk we fell. Yet how did we react? We were not content to crawl for the rest of our lives just because our first attempts at walking failed. Instead, we recognized that there was a new world waiting to be discovered; we got up and tried again until we achieved success.

> PERSONAL PAIN IS AN UNPLEASANT TEACHER, BUT AN EFFECTIVE ONE.

Challenge #4: Fear of Power Loss

Most of us enjoy power, position, authority, and the status symbols that go with them. It is human nature to expend massive amounts of effort in our quest to climb whichever ladder we happen to be on. The signs of this phenomenon are everywhere.

Business executives work eighty hours each week to attain higher positions. Politicians redraw the boundaries of their districts to consolidate their power and increase their influence. Some young married couples spend all their spare time working to gain the status symbols of a new car and big house, thinking that these will somehow add to their personal power, influence, and status.

In the world of organizational change, it is common for middle managers, supervisors, and union stewards initially to denounce proposed programs of labor-management cooperation. Why? Because they fear that their power bases will be lost if they begin to cooperate with the "other side." We should not be surprised when people resist ideas, programs, or other changes that they perceive will cause them to lose even the smallest amount of power, status, or control.

Challenge #5: Conflicting Programs, Policies, and Activities

Every new initiative or program automatically upsets an organization's status quo. It has to or it is not really a change. This means that at least some existing program, policy, or activity will be changed, postponed, or eliminated when a new program comes on line. This fact seems to escape many in organizational leadership as they continue to pile one new program on top of another without expecting any loss of productivity or effectiveness.

> ALL NEW PROGRAMS COMPETE FOR LIMITED RESOURCES AND MUST BE PRIORITIZED.

All new programs and change management efforts compete for limited resources. People, finances, technology, information, and time are required to implement even the simplest new initiative. Leaders would do well to prioritize all of their projects and then properly resource them—or simply wait for a more opportune time to implement at least some of them.

This is true of any area of life. My wife and I regularly discuss goals for improvement in our home life. Through the years we have focused on many issues, such as developing the talents of our four children, spending more quality time together, getting in shape, and slowing down the hectic pace of life, just to name a few. We often find that we are either trying to do too much with too few resources or that we are trying to accomplish two goals that are in direct conflict. We recently discovered that we had scheduled too many activities for the children in too short a period. The constant driving to piano lessons, karate classes, and football games frustrated us. These activities were in direct conflict with our goal of spending more quality time together. It was not until we had a family meeting to clarify our priorities and resolve that conflict that a "relative" peace returned to our home.

Challenge #6: Lack of Patience

Our world is filled with fast food, express lanes in grocery stores, and even Las Vegas-style drive-through weddings, performed while the bride and groom sit impatiently in their car. We surf through dozens of television channels in seconds. Merchants are open for business twenty-four hours a day, seven days a week, so customers can shop whenever they please. Of course, the instant gratification craze does not stop there. Throughout the world, credit card debt has grown exponentially. People gladly use their cards to get

> WE BECOME FRUSTRATED WHEN WE HAVE TO WAIT FOR ANYTHING TODAY.

what they want now and pay for it later, accepting—perhaps as a form of penance—the high rate of interest added to their bills each month.

Impatience has become part of our very souls. This often has some very painful consequences. Here's my own confession. When I go to restaurants, I hate waiting for soup to cool. It just takes too long. Sometimes I think that the cooks see me coming and turn their scalding cauldrons up another hundred degrees or so. Once served, I typically wait no more than fifteen seconds and then just dig in despite the steam swirling off the surface of the soup. The result of this folly is always the same: a severely burned tongue, which causes more delay than if I had waited longer in the first place.

Challenge #7: Poor Interpersonal Relationships

As stated earlier, each organization is in the business of relationships. The way in which people interact and relate largely determines the organization's success or failure. In reality, people within an organization either work together as a team, work independently, or work against each other. When employees work well together, it produces open communication, trust-based relationships, productive approaches to conflict resolution, joint problem solving and decision making, and a host of other positive outcomes. When they do not work well together or, in the worst case, work against each other, the results are completely opposite. Communication shuts down, trust is lost, conflicts go unresolved, problems are left to fester, and decisions are often delayed indefinitely. This is a real showstopper when it comes to organizational change and the pursuit of excellence at any level.

Interpersonal relationships must be strong enough to withstand the strain of change. Organizations that overlook this fact often try a wide variety of programs to enhance performance, but, sadly, they never work.

Challenge #8: Lack of Leadership Commitment

While it is difficult to comprehend the reason for its existence, this much is certain: The lack of commitment on the part of organizational leaders is the most difficult of the challenges to over-come. It is also the most damaging to an organization's growth and development. Leaders, by their very nature, must be committed to making whatever changes are needed for success. Their support is vital, especially in the early stages of the process. It is during this period that leaders initiate most of the action and keep the pro-cess moving forward by their investment of time, money, support, counsel, and other resources. A lack of leadership commitment undermines an organization's ability to compete and destroys any hope of employee participation in the change process. I have ob-served this many times over the past quarter century.

In the late 1980s I had the task of implementing a quality im-provement program in a company that made automotive parts. Initially it appeared that the organization was ready for change, but soon the top leader's lack of commitment to the process was revealed. At first the plant manager told his workforce about the importance of quality and safety in the workplace. Despite his zeal and use of all the latest buzz words, his employees were uninspired by his speech.

> THE MOST SENIOR EMPLOYEES WERE THE ONES WITH THE MOST SCARS ON THEIR HANDS AND ARMS.

A quick tour of the plant re-vealed the reason for their indiffer-ence. The machines, incredibly loud and virtually impossible to adjust for quality improvement, were all relics made in the 1940s. At unpredictable intervals, these mechanical volcanoes spewed hot oil onto the unsuspecting employees below. Some enterprising members of one department had made canopies from pieces of scrap cardboard to protect themselves from the constant shower of sludge that oozed from poorly maintained overhead lines. In ad-dition, the plant had no automated system for handling materials, which meant that employees had to physically carry each piece of razor sharp sheet metal from one machine to the next. It was easy to identify the most senior employees by the number of scars on their hands and arms.

The impact of this work environment on the company's bottom line was predictable. It suffered from low productivity, poor quality, and abysmal profitability. Further evidence of the chaos was seen in high rates of absenteeism, employee turnover, grievances, and injuries. Customer complaints were common, since error and rework delayed most product deliveries. This was a perfect location for a comprehensive change process, and with support from top management the employees were obviously ready to make great things happen.

> LEADERSHIP COMMITMENT IS THE KEY TO ANY SUCCESSFUL CHANGE PROCESS.

Unfortunately, things did not turn out that way for one simple reason. The plant manager's commitment to change was simply not there. Instead of apologizing for allowing the company to fall into disrepair, he gave heated lectures to employees on the need for *them* to build quality into *their* products. The manager scolded them for *their* lack of productivity and threatened them with job loss if *they* did not improve. All the while, he refused to invest the funds necessary to upgrade the machinery, provide safety equipment, and clean up the plant. He obviously was not committed to improve his organization, and his speeches did little to convince the employees otherwise. This was a sad but classic case of lose/lose/lose.

Leadership commitment is the key to any successful change process. Without it an organization has little more than a short-term program upon which to build its very uncertain future.

CHAPTER 5

Is Your Organization Programmed for Failure?

A program, by definition, has a distinct beginning and ending. Perhaps the best example of this involves the format of evening television shows. Just before the start of a program, we are treated to a barrage of quick highlights to pique our interest, and then the show begins. One hour later, it ends. And then? It's time for another program. In the quest for organizational success, things are much the same. Training programs, safety programs, diversity programs, productivity programs, and a host of others spring up with a great deal of fanfare, only to end a short time later.

One of the common program themes in recent years is quality improvement. These "new releases" often start with a passionate proclamation from company leaders about the need to implement such an important initiative. Executives and administrators declare that quality must be improved and pledge their deep commitment to this new mindset. Training seminars on quality push their way into the schedules of already busy managers and supervisors. Posters with catchy slogans like "Quality Is Everyone's Job" and "We Love Our Customers" magically appear throughout the workplace. Top managers, eager to help the effort succeed, leave the sanctuary of their corner offices and actually come out to where the work is being done. The program has begun . . .

With all of this momentum, not to mention the time and money being thrown at the issue, the program to improve quality may actually produce some positive results—temporarily. However, as with all programs, it will soon end. Why? In some organizations, corporate management cannot justify increased costs to their board, so the program is shut down. At other locations, the program to improve quality begins to slow production as workers actually watch for defects or rejects. This slowdown means that that delivery to customers is delayed, which is unacceptable to top management . . . so end of program. At yet another organization, labor and management relations break down over some issue unrelated to the change initiative, causing one side or the other to withhold their commitment to the program . . . so the program ends.

> THE NEW SLOGAN WAS QUALITY IS NO ONE'S JOB.

When the new initiative grinds to a halt, disillusioned employees begin a poster campaign of their own. Now bathroom walls and interoffice memos contain revised slogans like "Quality Is *No One's* Job" and "We *Leave* Our Customers." Soon the program is over and only one thing has really changed: management has lost credibility with employees and customers alike because they tried to use a program rather than a comprehensive process to improve quality.

Is It a Program or a New Way of Life?

It is often difficult to tell whether a newly launched effort is a new way of organizational life or just another program destined for failure. The following three indicators, however, will quickly help to tell the difference.

Indicator #1 – Low Levels of Involvement, Support, or Commitment

One of the most telling indicators is the amount of involvement that people, at all levels, have in the design and implementation of the initiative. People tend to ignore, resist, fear, or even sabotage programs and initiatives that they do not help to create. Without a sense of ownership, we tend to view new ideas from a distance, looking for flaws and asking, "What's in this for me?"

The issue of ownership cannot be overemphasized here. In training seminars, my associates and I often ask the participants a question that supports this point: *How many of you wash a rental car before returning it?* We have never seen a single hand go up in response. When asked to explain why, people clearly state that they do not wash the cars because *they do not own them.* In other words, they will pay to use the car, but their concern and commitment end there. Leaders who fail to comprehend the power of ownership sentence themselves to months of hard labor when they attempt to implement even the simplest change.

> WE DON'T WASH OUR RENTAL CARS FOR ONE SIMPLE REASON: WE DON'T OWN THEM.

The lesson here is simple. If you fail to involve the people around you in planning and implementing any significant undertaking, they will not view the program as their own. They may or may not participate in the program. Those who do participate will do so only as long as their best interests are served. You will find yourself having to do all of the work and still falling far short of your intended goal. If this describes the change initiative under your leadership, then you are in charge of a program, not a sustainable process. It is time for a change.

Indicator #2 – The Crisis of the Month

Hold it! This month's figures are in. People are upset. Productivity dropped. Rejects increased. Quality slipped. A grievance was filed. Are these causes for concern? Of course. Are these reasons for a drastic change program to be implemented? Of course . . . *not!*

Too many organizations launch major initiatives with nothing more than some random information as their impetus. We live in a world filled with those best described as "Chicken Little." In the classic children's story, Chicken Little is a neurotic baby chick that, when hit on the head by a falling acorn, promptly begins to run through its world squawking, "The sky is falling!" Too often change programs start because of an isolated problem or temporary crisis. When we use Chicken Little's approach to problem analysis, we also get his results. Lots of squawking and wasted energy, but very little progress.

Similar to this is what is known as the flavor-of-the-month program. These are promoted by leaders who, like ice cream shops, offer a different flavor each month, seemingly for variety's sake. One month the special is safety, the next month it's quality, followed by productivity, cost savings, and more. Some of these fine folks even boast about the large variety of flavors (programs) that have been offered in the recent past. For some strange reason they see the constant changing of direction as a virtue rather than a wasteful vice.

Obviously, the crisis, flavor, or fad approach makes little sense. Each results in short-term programs with few long-term gains.

Indicator #3 – Multiple, Disjointed Initiatives

Some organizations attempt to run multiple, unrelated programs at the same time. If an organization has a constant stream of initiatives that are not directly linked to its mission, then it is a sure bet that it is using a program approach to change management as opposed to implementing a long-term process. These programs frequently conflict with one another for time, meeting space, money, and support from leaders. And amazingly these programs are often unrelated to the organization's vision, mission, and/or values. Like parasites, these programs hang on, draining life from their host while giving back little in the way of true value.

Short-Term Programs

A wise man once said that there was nothing new under the sun. This is certainly true when it comes to change management. Throughout the world, a relatively small number of topics are converted into short-term programs each year. Although each has the ability to improve an organization when implemented *as part of a comprehensive process for change*, none has the power to transform the organization by itself. Let's look at some of the most common program topics and why they are not able to truly change an organization's culture.

CHAPTER 6

Common Programs . . . and Why They Fail

Organizations that attempt to achieve long-term success by implementing short-term programs always fall short of their goals. The following are some of the most common program topics and fundamental reasons why they fail.

Motivation Programs

A leader who selects motivation as a primary organizational development strategy assumes a great deal. Specifically, he or she concludes that employees and/or volunteers have everything they need to be productive, that interpersonal relationships are optimal, and that everyone involved lacks only one essential element for success: motivation.

Once this assumption is made, the path forward is easy to see. Hire a motivational speaker—any professional athlete, coach, or actor, will do—and have them inspire employees with stories of last-second victories and the joys of the journey. What could possibly be wrong with that? Actually, plenty. While the speeches may be exciting, they often provide a short-term, caffeine-type boost that wears off and leaves listeners feeling worse than before.

The reason is simple: as soon as the thrill of the moment fades, the employees realize that their problems still exist.

What good is a blast of external motivation for employees who have no new tools to address their real-life problems? Regardless of how much they enjoyed the speaker, the workers actually lose motivation when they realize that their leaders have failed to take genuine *action* to resolve the real issues.

Employee Suggestion Programs

For years, employee suggestion boxes have been prominent features on the landscape of the organizational terrain. While the concept of gathering employee input is a good one, the process leaves much to be desired. Suggestion programs should never be the primary means of gathering employee ideas. They provide one-way, rather than two-way, communication. This causes misunderstanding and misinterpretation of an employee's ideas.

These programs are plagued with other problems as well. For example, many suggestions have not been researched sufficiently before submission. Rather than bringing forth well-conceived plans for change, employees often see problems and suggest that management or administration do something about them. This creates additional work for managers and supervisors who have little time to follow up on what may or may not be good ideas. The problems with suggestion programs don't end there. In the worst-case scenario, good suggestions are stolen from the person who actually submitted them, causing distrust and employee apathy.

Suggestion programs occasionally reward quantity rather than quality, which results in some strange ideas indeed. As a new employee in an automotive factory in the late 1970s, I was introduced to our company's year-round "ten suggestions" program by a cynical senior employee. He explained how it worked: the employees ignored the program for eleven and a half months and then submitted their ten suggestions just before the December 15 deadline. The reason? Just before Christmas the company would present a frozen turkey as a reward to every employee who had submitted ten suggestions during the previous year. Naturally, at the last moment the corporate office was flooded with thousands of suggestions, most of which were worthless.

> ONE SUGGESTION WAS TO CUT HOLES IN THE ROOF TO LET THE HOT AIR OUT!

This senior coworker was a master of abusing the system and proudly showed me a copy of his ten suggestions for the year. They included such novel ideas as "cutting holes in the roof to let the hot air out in the summer," followed by "drilling holes in the floor to drain away any rain water that comes in through the holes in the roof." Based on how the program was run, the reward of a turkey still seems very appropriate.

Clearly there is a need to obtain suggestions, ideas, and input, but there is a better way to handle the process, as we will explore throughout this book.

Creating New Structures and Reporting Relationships

On occasion, organizations need to restructure and change reporting relationships to optimize performance. It is folly, however, for any company, government, nonprofit, or school system to make these changes without knowing if the change will actually solve existing problems. Creating new structures and changing reporting relationships are incredibly disruptive and costly. They create massive amounts of potential confusion while offering little in terms of real organizational optimization. At times, this sort of change actually hides the true issues and problems, rather than exposing and solving them.

One of our past clients, a small assembly firm with one hundred employees, experienced the perennial problems of low product quality and high employee turnover. This company was owned and operated by two men in their late forties. When we first met, one was in charge of production and the other was in charge of sales and marketing. Each had a corner office in their small corporate headquarters and rarely walked out to where their employees were doing the actual work. Instead, they attempted to run things from computer printouts, sales and production figures, and an occasional accident report.

After a thorough assessment of their operation, we recommended that they begin to focus on employee relations, leadership effectiveness, operational redesign, and increased communication throughout their company. While this dynamic duo made a few feeble attempts to implement the recommended changes, they rejected our advice and implemented their own strategy for success.

> EVERY YEAR THE TWO OWNERS SIMPLY EXCHANGED JOBS— RATHER THAN ADDRESS THE REAL PROBLEMS.

Here is what they did. Approximately every twelve months the men would simply exchange jobs. They would loudly and proudly announce to the employees that great new things were happening at their company, and then they would switch titles and move across the hall into the other's office! In some strange way they saw this as progress. But the workforce saw it for what it really was: a useless exercise that ignored the real problems plaguing the organization. After several years of that organizational madness, the owners finally decided to make some foundational changes in their operation and have since begun to prosper.

Quality Promotion Programs

As we noted earlier, leaders have learned the importance of providing quality in their goods and services. This revelation has led to numerous quality improvement programs in business, education, government, and health care operations. These programs go by many different names: total quality management, quality improvement programs, statistical process control programs, and many others. The focus on quality is a great thing. The problem comes, however, when these programs are forced from the top down with little input from the people who actually have to implement them. This often leaves leaders fighting the battles for quality improvement by themselves, with employees passively watching from the wings. An even worse scenario occurs when leaders demand quality—as long as it does not slow productivity or cost any money. Employees quickly see that approach as hypocrisy.

It takes all members of an organization working together to achieve true quality improvement through a new way of life rather than through a short-term program. This lifestyle change can only be built in organizations where high-quality relationships have been created from top to bottom and side to side.

Productivity Incentive Programs

For years, business leaders in the manufacturing world have tried to motivate employees to be more productive by offering financial incentives for each completed unit of production. This has, at times, encouraged increased production, but often at the expense of quality.

Employees have always been quick to learn ways to beat any productivity incentive system. I recall a coworker who was responsible for operating an industrial laser in an automotive assembly plant. He was required to place a power steering housing into a machine, push two buttons to run the laser inside of the housing, remove the housing, and repeat the process hundreds of times each day. Each time he pushed the buttons a counter on his machine would advance, crediting him with one completed unit of production. Under this system, the more parts he ran, the more money he made.

On days that he was particularly upset with the department supervisor, the worker would modify his production routine slightly. He would simply leave the housing in his machine and run the laser repeatedly inside the same part. This did three things. First, since his pay was based on production, he received money for work that he did not do. Second, it created a headache for the managers and accountants who could never figure out what happened to all of those extra parts that appeared on the monthly production run sheets. Third, it compromised the quality of the parts that were run through the process multiple times.

Productivity incentives can be beneficial, but only when there is an honest and mutual labor-management commitment to the organization's success.

Efficiency Improvement Programs

Every organization should look for ways to be more efficient. It is often helpful to have someone from the outside identify blind spots that may be missed by those too close to the situation. Misuse of this practice comes, however, when outsiders are invited in for a few quick observations and then allowed to make recommendations to dismantle entire components of the operation, lay off employees, or change the organization's basic mission.

Too often, "efficiency" experts recommend staff cuts rather than additions and fail to spend sufficient time with local personnel to truly understand the complex issues that face the organization. The true experts in efficiency are the managers, supervisors, engineers, and employees that work with the processes every day. A much better philosophical approach to efficiency improvement is to engage as many people as possible in meaningful dialogue about process improvements and then work with them to implement the recommendations.

The Bottom Line on Programs

Short-term programs simply are not the answer to the long-term success of any organization. What is needed is a comprehensive, systematic process that begins with new vision and values and then develops the human assets necessary for success. Such a process is built upon fundamental truths and not upon faulty assumptions, as we will discover in the next chapter.

CHAPTER 7

Three Faulty Assumptions about Change Management

As human beings, we adjust to changes around us each and every day. In fact, we spend a fair amount of time consciously or subconsciously planning to optimize the quality of our lives. For example, before we select our clothing for any given day, we check the weather report to determine what will be the most appropriate. Cold, rain, snow, heat, all impact our choices. In like manner, we adjust our budgets to coincide with short-term or long-term changes in income. As parents, we change countless aspects of our lives when our children are born, go to school, and then eventually leave the nest.

The point is that we all practice the art of managing change most of our lives. This then begs the question: If individuals have so much experience managing change, then why do organizations, comprised of these same individuals, struggle so much with this issue? Over the years, I have found that leaders often fail to manage change successfully because of three faulty assumptions.

Faulty Assumption #1:
Change management will be
quick and inexpensive

Some organizations refuse to take the time necessary to prepare their people for change. "Full speed ahead" is their motto, even though they are headed off a cliff. Corporate cultures, good or bad, take years to create and improving them cannot be accomplished overnight. The notion that an organization can change its vision, values, or fundamental approach to operations in just a few quick, easy steps is unrealistic. The process is more art than science. While some improvements may be seen early, many take months or even years to manifest fully.

Others seem to want something for nothing and are therefore unwilling to spend significant time or money to create a positive corporate culture. I occasionally get requests from such companies. Their cries for help usually sound something like this:

> There are some big problems at our firm. We have a large group of people here who are not working together; no one communicates; we have high grievances, high turnover, and low morale. Can you help us?

So far, so good. After some further discussion, the issues of time and money naturally come up. Then it gets interesting.

> Well, we don't want to take people off their jobs at all for any training, and we sure don't want them to go off-site. Way too expensive. By the way, we have put a couple thousand dollars in our budget for employee development. We won't want to spend more than that. We can have the employees come in before work starts in the morning for the training—you know, on

their own time. The storage area in the back can be converted into a classroom if we move some boxes and chairs around.

I have heard these ramblings many times in the past from people painfully stuck between two opposing philosophies. On one hand, they want their employees or volunteers to be more effective, which will translate into greater success for the organization. On the other hand, they struggle to believe that these same people are worth the investment needed to make it happen.

> SOME MANAGERS WANT POSITIVE CHANGE, BUT STRUGGLE TO BELIEVE THAT THEY SHOULD INVEST IN THEIR PEOPLE TO MAKE IT HAPPEN.

With enough coaxing, some commit the resources needed and good things happen. Sadly, many follow the path that seems easier, quicker, and certainly cheaper. They somehow talk themselves out of doing the right thing and simply hope for a better day. This approach begins a downward spiral of degenerating performance and relationships. The leaders soon view the people around them as the cause of their problems rather than as essential parts of the solution. When this happens the decision makers panic and vainly attempt to force better performance rather than build the team. Predictably, workers (since they are viewed as the problem) are first browbeaten, then threatened, and finally laid off in vain attempts to reverse the downward trends. Those employees who remain become preoccupied with their own survival and, rather than playing the game to win, begin trying not to lose. Innovation, creative problem solving, and extra effort are hard to find since no one wants to take any sort of risk.

Creating a positive organizational culture takes time and money to accomplish. There are no shortcuts and no way around these facts.

Faulty Assumption #2:
Organizational relationships are strong
enough to stand the strain of change

America's automotive manufacturing giants, such as General Motors, and their satellite industries have tried for years to implement cultural improvement programs, but with limited success. The reasons vary from location to location. These extensive and expensive programs generally failed, however, due to poor labor-management relationships and mistrust on both sides.

> UNRESOLVED DISAGREEMENT RESULTS IN WEAKNESS AND FAILURE.

Despite these failings, for decades General Motors seemed invincible. Certainly its massive size would protect it against problems caused by poor relationships. Every day automobiles came rolling off the assembly lines and money was being made. That had to be progress, right? Not exactly. Remember, agreement between two factions results in dynamic power and success. Disagreement between two factions, therefore, results in weakness and failure—and will continue to do so until it is reconciled, which, in the case of GM, never really happened.

Like a poorly tended fire, the fractured relationship between General Motors and the United Auto Workers Union smoldered just under the surface for years before finally bursting into flame during the summer of 1998. A disagreement between the two sides sent the union over the edge and began a destructive chain of events that rocked the country. Union officials chose to strike at some supplier plants rather than to organize a nationwide strike. This strategic move effectively shut down General Motors' operations while minimizing the union's financial exposure. The cost to the company was a staggering 1.2 billion dollars in second quarter profits alone!

Eventually the strike was ended and contracts were subsequently signed, but at what cost? Clearly the leaders of General Motors and their union counterparts treated each other as enemies rather than as allies before and during contract negotiations. Whenever battle lines like this are drawn in the corporate world there can be no winners—only survivors. If anyone ever doubts the value of productive relationships to an organization's bottom line, I suggest that we start with the figure of 1.2 billion dollars, and go from there. Lose/lose/lose.

The lesson here is clear, even though for some it seems to be hidden while in plain view. The quality of our relationships with others in and around our organization will largely determine whether we survive and prosper or struggle and fail. The General Motors scenario is played out countless times each year as smaller businesses, ministries, and civic organizations start up, sputter, and then unceremoniously shut down. In fact, a majority of new business start-ups fail within the first sixty months of operation. While there can be many contributing factors, the first place I would look to find the cause is the area of relationships.

At some point we must stop viewing organizations with such a "charts and graphs" mentality and begin to see them more from a human perspective. Remember, regardless of what type of organization you belong to, you are in the *people* business. Despite the addition of new technology, computers, and robotics, an organization's success or failure will always depend on human factors.

Governments, businesses, churches, and hospitals count on people at every level for their very existence. People supply these organizations with raw materials. People make their products and provide services. People must attract other people to purchase or use the goods and services, and so on. It is all about people and their relationships with others. Organizations achieve maximum prosperity only as long as the interpersonal relationships among their people remain productive, trust-based, and supportive.

Faulty Assumption #3:
Employees and volunteers understand
the reason why change is needed

Unless the details of a change management process are explained *before* it begins, the people involved will probably not understand—and may even resist—the effort. Production managers have failed miserably in their attempts to have employees monitor quality performance with statistical process control charts. Why? Because management failed to communicate how the initiative could improve product quality and therefore customer satisfaction, which would in turn provide job security for the employees. Big mistake. Remember, people are much more likely to be supportive if they receive an honest and timely explanation before the change actually occurs.

By avoiding these assumptions, leaders will avoid many pitfalls and build their corporate culture on some rock-solid foundations.

PART TWO

Building a
Positive Culture

CHAPTER 8

Foundations for Building a Positive Culture

J ust as there are faulty assumptions to avoid when creating a positive corporate culture, likewise there are solid truths to embrace. To begin with, individuals and organizations alike need more than a quick fix to reach their optimum levels of performance. Instead, they need a complete, comprehensive process of renewal. As with all building projects, the change process starts with some strong foundations.

Foundation #1:
Commitment to a Long-Term Process

Commitment is an extremely powerful word when used in any professional or personal context. For example, during our wedding ceremony my wife and I made vows to remain together *forever*. Our vows were not made to sustain our commitment during the honeymoon. That was the easy part. We voiced our promise to stick together through the tests and trials that assault every marriage long after the honeymoon has ended. We saw marriage as a life-long journey, not a two-year contract with renewable options. It made sense to approach our relationship as a marathon, not a sprint.

Other commitments soon followed the wedding, as my life began to change in many wonderful ways. The next decade saw a restoration of relationship with my extended family, a new relationship with my Creator, new business opportunities, and the birth of our four children. Each change required a deep, long-term commitment to realize its full benefits in my life, especially during times of adversity.

> EACH CHANGE REQUIRES DEEP, LONG-TERM COMMITMENT TO REALIZE ITS FULL BENEFITS.

In the first few years I questioned whether I could be a good husband and father. The shift from "me" thinking to "we" thinking took longer than I had expected. On occasion I would long for the freedom that I previously had enjoyed, especially once the children came along and "relaxing" meant five minutes alone in the bathroom rather than long weekends fishing with my friends. There is a temptation for anyone, or any organization, going through change to reflect on the good old days—and perhaps to want to return to them. I am glad that I didn't. Whatever sacrifices I may have made are nothing compared to the joy that my family brings to me.

So it is with our businesses, ministries, governments, and other organizations. Without commitment to a long-term process, change efforts quickly falter. At the first sign of trouble someone will want to quit and return to the good old days. Perhaps people forget that if the old days had been so "good," the change wouldn't have been initiated in the first place.

Remember that the long-term approach to change management is much like a marriage: it is best entered into with eyes wide open and is sustained when the people involved make unbreakable vows of commitment to one another. This commitment represents a new and better way of life for everyone, without the option of turning back. In an organizational setting, a long-term commitment ensures follow-through on the change process, regardless of the challenges.

Foundation #2:
High Levels of Involvement during Times of Change

Virtually every decision involving a cultural change process will require follower support in order to be successfully implemented. Therefore, one of the most important lessons for leaders to learn comes in the following formula:

Meaningful Involvement = Support and Commitment

In other words, if we want our ideas to be embraced and supported by others, then we must involve them in the decision-making process *before* a final decision is made. The reason for the high level of involvement is simple, yet compelling. People support what they help create. We tend to take care of things that are ours. Remember, we don't wash rental vehicles for one fundamental reason: we don't own them. If an initiative needs support and commitment from others to succeed, then it is vital to involve them early and often in the design and implementation process. This is much more than an attempt by leaders to be "nice." It is a precise strategy for enhanced performance and increased competitiveness. Involved followers are more committed to the vision and will sacrifice to see it accomplished.

Foundation #3:
High-Quality Relationships throughout the Organization

Positive change cannot be dictated, mandated, or forced upon people. It must be presented in a way that creates a desire for change in the hearts of those impacted by the initiative. Without question, positive change occurs most rapidly and efficiently in an atmosphere of trust, openness, and supportive relationships.

> THE QUALITY OF INTERPERSONAL RELATIONSHIPS PLAYS AN IMMENSE ROLE IN AN ORGANIZATION'S SUCCESS OR FAILURE.

Mature leaders realize that they cannot do it all by themselves, despite society's constant barrage of messages to the contrary. Through the years, popular songs have captured the world's self-centered approach to life and success. Musical hits like "I Did It My Way" and "I Gotta Be Me" may be entertaining, but they aren't very accurate. In this life, not much happens without the support of others. In addition, it is virtually impossible to gain this kind of support on a long-term basis without developing and maintaining productive relationships. I am not referring to some sort of bizarre corporate commune where employees hold hands and sing the company song to get motivated for work every morning. I *am* saying, however, that the quality of the interpersonal relationships in an organization plays an immense role in its ultimate success or failure.

For the past quarter century I have studied a wide variety of organizations to determine what causes them either to prosper or to stumble. Amazingly, the primary cause of low organizational effectiveness is not lack of funds, outdated equipment, or anything else related to its overall operation. Instead, the primary obstacle to success is the poor interpersonal relationships within the organization itself.

> LEADERS OFTEN KNOW WHAT THEIR FOLLOWERS DO, BUT LITTLE ABOUT WHO THEY ARE.

Leaders in the corporate world often have a stronger relationship with their work than with their workers. It is common for managers, supervisors, and administrators to know what their followers *do,* but little about who they *are.* Followers often know even less about their leaders. In these situations, tasks become more important than relationships. Sadly, leaders who spend little time on relationships never obtain their followers' full commitments to change. I have seen scores of worthwhile projects in businesses, churches, educational institutions, and governments fail for that one simple reason. Conversely, I have seen countless organizations succeed because their leaders took time to build the relationships necessary for positive change to occur. Once the positive relationships are built, the actual work itself can be accomplished with much greater efficiency and—believe it or not—enjoyment.

CHAPTER 9

The Biggest Picture: How Things Actually Get Done

I n the next few chapters we will explore how organizations actually get things done. First, we must clarify some terms.

What's in a Name?

Terms such as *vision*, *mission*, *values*, *goals*, and *objectives* can be confusing. This is not because the words are difficult to comprehend, but because they are often used interchangeably. One organization calls its overall statement of purpose a vision statement, another calls it a mission statement, and so on. Some companies set "goals," while others establish "objectives" for their employees to pursue. Fortunately, it doesn't matter which terms are used as long as *everyone* in the organization understands what the terms actually mean.

Although it sounds like corporate blasphemy, I believe there is little value in statements of vision or mission, or even in written goals, in and of themselves. Here's why: Throughout the world, there are thousands of mission statements being used for little more than dust collectors on executives' walls. In reality, the ultimate reason to have statements of vision, mission, goals, etc. is to insure that all people involved in the organization understand how their work contributes to the whole.

How Things Get Done

Organizations are birthed with vision. They begin to grow when the vision is translated into an achievable mission that all members of the organization can embrace as their own. The organization matures as the statement of mission is subdivided into clearly defined goals, which are then further broken into prioritized projects. The final growth takes place when each project is divided into tasks that are carried out by individual members of the organization.

In theory, when all members of the organization achieve their individual tasks, then each project will be accomplished, which will lead to the achievement of the goals, which results in mission accomplished. Naturally, there are many opportunities for problems to arise that hinder productivity. By having a systematic process such as this to follow, an organization has the greatest chance of success.

Each step in the process (except for vision, because it begins the process) is linked to those above and below it. The components closest to the bottom provide increasing amounts of details about what is to be done. Properly conceived and implemented, this type of organized approach causes each member of the organization to understand the importance of his or her contribution to the vision, guarantees accountability, and promotes growth. It is truly how things get done.

Step by Step

The following overview of each component explains their interrelationships and importance for organizational success.

Vision

The vision is the overarching picture of what an organization will do or become. Its primary value is in motivating others to join the organization for its worthy cause. An organization's vision comes only from its founders or from new top leaders interested in changing the organization's direction. The vision typically represents the heart and mind of the leader(s) as it relates to his or her organization. The various words, terms, and phrases that comprise the vision must be translated and recorded as a statement of mission in order for others to embrace it.

Mission

The statement of mission adds detail to the vision. It is a much clearer description of what must be done for the organization to succeed. The primary value of a mission statement is to focus everyone's efforts toward a common purpose. The statement must be subdivided into primary goals in order to become a reality. Mission statements come from the top members of the organization.

Primary Goals

Primary goals are used to clarify further what must be done to accomplish an organization's mission. Primary goals are actually subdivisions of the mission that are assigned to key individuals. Some organizations may refer to these primary goals as objectives, which is perfectly acceptable. Regardless of which term is used, the key to success is for these primary goals to be written in language that is easy to understand and then communicated to those who will be accountable for their fulfillment. Primary goals identify specific targets and measurements for the accomplishment of the mission. Goals are set mutually by those at the top of the organization and by other leaders below them. These goals must then be subdivided into prioritized projects in order to be achieved.

Prioritized Projects

Things get very exciting at this stage, as all of the planning that went into the vision, mission, and primary goals is now translated into specific activities. The vision identified the ultimate destination, the statement of mission set the course, and the primary goals focused attention on what really counts.

Each goal now becomes the foundation for one or more projects that are then assigned to a group or individual that takes responsibility for their completion. At this stage, those responsible for the project must have a great deal of input on exactly how the project will be undertaken, what resources are needed, and how long it will take to finish. Once the projects have been identified and prioritized, they are subdivided for the final time into individual tasks, which are then assigned to people willing and able to see them accomplished.

Individual Tasks

Each project will generally have multiple individual tasks involved in its completion. The person responsible for the project will either perform these tasks or assign them to others. Individual tasks are the fundamental building blocks in the achievement of any mission. They are the daily duties that employees and volunteers attend to each day. Making phone calls, entering data into computers, running equipment, solving problems, and attending meetings are individual tasks that combine to complete the broader projects.

It is very important that each person understand how his or her daily tasks help the organization achieve its ultimate mission. Those who fail to comprehend this connection often become discouraged and feel as if their efforts are meaningless. This scenario must be avoided if the mission is to be accomplished in an excellent and timely manner.

Many years ago some creative songwriter came up with a catchy tune that detailed how our bones are connected to one another. Countless people bounced through their days singing, "The foot bone's connected to the ankle bone, the ankle bone's connected to the leg bone, the leg bone's connected to the knee bone, the knee bone's connected to the thigh bone," and so on. I always think of that tune when teaching people about the importance and interconnection of each person's contribution to the mission. It is too easy to forget that what each person in an organization does is linked to what others do. Perhaps some new songwriter can put this to music: "The task is connected to the project, the project is connected to the primary goal, the goal is connected to the mission, the mission is connected to the vision." Our new song may not become a number one hit, but it certainly will help organizations realize how to be effective.

Detailed Performance Standards and Timelines

The final element that must be considered relates to how and when a task will be completed. For every task that is performed in an organization, there is a proper way to perform it. It takes detailed performance standards and timelines to insure that each task is done correctly and on time.

Employees, volunteers, and other followers must know who is to be involved in the task, what is to be done, where it is to be done, and have some basic understanding of how each task is to be completed. Many tasks need to have detailed performance standards in writing to guarantee that there are no misunderstandings or variation in how they are accomplished. The final piece of necessary information is a timeline of when each task should be done.

Leaders who fail to clarify these standards and timelines are often disappointed at the poor performance of their followers. But in the absence of clear instructions and written standards, most people will simply make up their own. This sort of free thinking is great if you are brainstorming new methods for capturing market share; it can be devastating, however, when employees begin to guess at quality standards, delivery deadlines, and other customer-related issues.

Communication Is Key

In the best organizations, leaders at each level also explain *why* the task is to be done so that each person understands how his or her efforts link with all others. Here is a very important point that we will build upon in later chapters. Once leaders have provided proper instructions about goals, projects, and individual tasks, they should be very open to employee suggestions about *how* to get these things accomplished. After an initial learning period, employees and volunteers obtain new perspectives about their work that may go well beyond that of their leaders. For this reason, leaders must communicate with and listen to employees, especially during times of rapid and unpredictable change. This approach releases the power of agreement in a profound way. That is how things get done, as we will see in the following case study.

CHAPTER 10

CASE STUDY

Manufacturing

Dow Corning Corporation

F rom its very first day, the Dow Corning manufacturing plant
in Elizabethtown, Kentucky was plagued with problems.
The only thing worse than its productivity was its labor-management
relationships. This unionized manufacturing site employed
260 people. In the first few years of operation the union went on
strike twice, costing the company nearly three million dollars.
Something obviously needed to change. But what?

In the early 1980s a number of Dow Corning employees—
including Ralph Reed, plant manager; Burnett Kelly, manager
of employee relations; Tony Singer, human relations director;
Dick Hazleton, corporate executive; and members of the union
committee, led by J. R. Vessels—got involved in a transformation
process for the plant. As part of the plan, I was asked to help
design a cultural change process specifically for that location.
Together we developed a unique approach to change that transformed the Elizabethtown operation into a world-class workplace.
The process that we created became a model for success at other
Dow Corning plants and many other organizations throughout the

world. It continues to inspire leaders to this day. Looking back, the renewal of the plant was no small task, considering that productivity, profitability, and quality were all extremely low. At the same time, conflict between labor and management was extremely high and communication was either very limited or extremely hostile. Lose/lose/lose.

Our initial assessment showed that the plant was losing popularity with customers and corporate officers alike. In fact, the entire operation was in real danger of being shut down if something didn't change. The many years of low productivity and high levels of labor-management strife had nearly convinced the corporate executives to invest their resources in other locations.

> THE ENTIRE OPERATION WAS IN DANGER OF BEING SHUT DOWN IF SOMETHING DIDN'T CHANGE.

On the surface, the roadblocks to success seemed insurmountable. Here are just a few examples: All of the managers were highly educated urbanites sent from the corporate headquarters in Michigan to supervise the local workers. In sharp contrast, the production-level employees had been born and raised in the surrounding hills of Kentucky. While some of them had graduated from high school, few had gone to college. There were other outward differences as well. Managers wore white shirts and dark ties. Workers wore blue uniforms. Managers spoke with Midwestern accents, while virtually all of the workers spoke with accents common to that region. These differences had pushed the people who worked there into two separate cliques—"us" and "them." The differences between the groups seemed too great to overcome; but with no viable alternative, we set out to change the culture.

After several days on site, we concluded that the plant had *nearly* everything it needed to succeed. It had plenty of space, good equipment, competent employees at all levels, customer demand for its products, and more. So what was lacking? Productive relationships. The project began, therefore, with one foundational belief—i.e., that the best way to improve bottom-line performance was first to improve relationships, from top to bottom and side to side. Using this philosophy as our guide, we encouraged the managers of the Elizabethtown operation to do something that few of their predecessors had tried: to talk *with* their union counterparts and other employees instead of talking *at* them.

A New Day

It was decided that for maximum progress to be made all employees needed to have a complete understanding of where the plant was going and how it hoped to get there. The first step in this process was to open the lines of communication. Each morning the two top managers, Reed and Singer, would walk through the plant, greet their coworkers, and ask them how they felt about their jobs, the company, and even the type of leadership they were receiving. These leaders were determined to learn about the hopes and fears of the other employees.

At first, people were hesitant to speak freely about their concerns, and many tried to avoid talking with the "bosses." After several weeks, however, things began to change. Many workers actually began to look forward to conversing with their leaders. Once it became clear that these men genuinely cared about the organization and the people who worked there, employees began to respond with improved work performance. Why were Reed and Singer successful? Because they discovered the power of becoming personally involved with the members of their team. They found areas of common interest and built upon

> AT FIRST, PEOPLE WERE HESITANT TO SPEAK FREELY ABOUT THEIR CONCERNS.

them. This simple approach to leadership began to unleash the power of agreement. It never fails!

Through the increased communication, staff and employees at the Elizabethtown plant discovered that they had much more in common than in conflict. The primary concern they shared was the real possibility of unemployment if plant performance did not dramatically improve. This gave managers and union employees a universal enemy to rally against: job loss! It also gave them a common goal: to improve their organization for the benefit of everyone who worked there.

However, even with the common threat to their livelihoods, it was soon obvious that not all members of the organization wanted to work together. Doubters on both sides wanted to see some results before they made a full commitment to the change process.

We knew that communication was crucial to the success of the plan, so we took every opportunity to communicate the vision, mission, and desired core values. Plant leaders continually talked about what type of culture they wanted and how everyone would benefit from the change. While much of this information was transmitted during informal communication with employees, management also formally declared their commitment to improve operations in every staff meeting. In response

> DOUBTERS ON BOTH SIDES WANTED TO SEE SOME RESULTS BEFORE MAKING A FULL COMMITMENT TO THE CHANGE PROCESS.

to the challenges before them, they developed a comprehensive mission statement that encompassed their six most critical business issues, their operating philosophy and principles, and their total commitment to teamwork. The Dow Corning leaders made sure that their statement was easy for all employees to understand, retain, and apply to their daily jobs. It was called their "mission statement" at the time, but it was actually much more than that. It included *what* they wanted to achieve, *how* they wanted to achieve it, and *which* business issues were most critical.

> Elizabethtown Mission Statement: [To] Demonstrate continuous improvement in team excellence as a high-quality, low-cost supplier who satisfies our customers' needs in a safe, productive, and waste-free manner.

For months, company leaders recited this statement to employees every chance they could. Soon workers were able to remember the vital business concerns that became known as the "Key Six": safety, quality, cost, productivity, supply (to customers), and reduction of waste. After a short while, each employee was able to use these six concerns to analyze and solve complex problems that previously would have halted production. They soon were able to make management-level decisions by focusing on what was truly important to the plant's success—the Key Six.

Trouble in Paradise

Within six months it was obvious that employees grasped the mission and mentally embraced the concept of having a unified workplace. However, embracing the concept and putting it into practice are two different things. The next part of our plan, therefore, was to build productive relationships among the 260 employees. Remember, these were the same managers, supervisors, and employees whose poor work performance and lack of teamwork had nearly ruined the company. Our plan for unifying the workplace started with a three-way partnership between management, local union leaders, and members of my staff. Together we examined a wide variety of subjects to include in a comprehensive training program for all employees. We eventually selected a core of topics that included leadership, teamwork, communication, trust building, and team problem solving.

Our initial training session was a memorable one. In an initial effort to build productive relationships at the highest levels of the plant, we designed a team-building workshop for management and their union counterparts. At the opening of our first session, I silently questioned the wisdom of such a gathering. The managers all sat on one side of the training room while the union leaders sat on the other. There was no eye contact. There were no smiles. It looked grim; but at that point there was no turning back.

In our first exercise, I asked participants to locate a person from the other group whom they knew little about. The assignment was to interview that person using some questions—unrelated to work—that I provided. The participants immediately responded to my instructions with disbelief. They looked shocked to think that they were being asked to cross the invisible barrier that ran down the center of the room and actually engage in positive dialogue with someone from the "other side." It was amusing to watch grown men try to cope with the uncomfortable situation. Each tried in vain to disappear from sight. Some shuffled their feet, some cleaned nonexistent spots on their glasses, and others suddenly developed an intense interest in the notebooks that had been placed on the tables. I felt as though I was the chaperon at a junior high school party watching as the boys and girls breathlessly waited for someone to ask for the first dance.

> ALL OF THE MANAGERS SAT ON ONE SIDE OF THE ROOM AND ALL OF THE UNION LEADERS SAT ON THE OTHER.

Finally one brave soul rose from his seat and called a cool invitation to a former adversary across the room. Mercifully, the invitation was accepted; the duo walked together from the room to a quiet place in the lobby.

The ice was broken! Other managers and union leaders slowly began to form pairs and ask each other the series of simple questions. After a brief period of guarded conversation, they began to share more openly about families, hobbies, personal goals, and the high points of their lives. I watched in grateful amazement as men pulled family photographs from their wallets and showed them to their new friends. Although I had given instructions for the interviewing assignment to be completed in thirty minutes, they didn't seem to care about the time limit. Once they started, these former enemies didn't want to stop talking with each other!

When I finally brought the entire group back together, I was amazed at the transformation that had taken place. They were smiling and joking and obviously much more at ease than when the workshop began. Many of them actually sat with the person whom they had interviewed, which destroyed the invisible barrier that was in the room earlier. When the entire group had finally reassembled, I asked them to identify common interests they had discovered during the interviews. What followed was an absolute clinic on how to build a team.

Union leaders and managers alike divulged the issues that gave true meaning to their lives. They talked about their spouses and children, their faith in God, their love for their country, and their desire for financial security. They shared their goals of a productive retirement and peace of mind. Many excitedly spoke about how they enjoyed fishing, hunting, golf, and other forms of recreation. By the end of the exercise these fine people discovered the truth that had been hidden from them for so long: those on both sides had a great deal

> ONCE THEY STARTED, THESE FORMER ENEMIES DIDN'T WANT TO STOP TALKING WITH EACH OTHER!

in common, and by agreeing to work together they could achieve both their personal and corporate goals. This one simple exercise opened a new era for their organization.

During the next few years, we trained each employee at the plant in a full range of interpersonal skills, including leadership, teamwork, communications, listening, trust building, and problem solving. In turn, these new skills laid a foundation for open dialogue and caused positive relationships to develop among workers at every level. As trust developed, so did more open lines of communication. This open communication resulted in better problem identification, analysis, and resolution, which resulted in improved work performance and a much more positive work environment. As this process took root, employees at all levels brought forth many innovative ideas to help the plant become a model not only for the rest of the corporation but also for organizations around the world. The results, as you are about to see, were amazing!

The Bottom Line

My team and I had the pleasure of working with the Elizabethtown operation for over seven years. During that time, their plant operated for more than three million man-hours without a single lost-time injury. In addition, they delivered products to customers on or before the delivery date more than 96 percent of the time. The multimillion dollar operation's fixed costs were reduced by over 7 percent. The rate of productivity rose by more than 6 percent. Manufacturing process waste was reduced by more than 25 percent. A 40 percent reduction in final rejects sent their quality ratings skyrocketing. As a wonderful byproduct of this success, the vast majority of employees and managers actually enjoyed coming to work. They were proud to be part of something so positive! This was an amazing example of win/win/win!

A True Turnaround

This case study should motivate every champion of change, even those facing seemingly insurmountable odds. Why? Because unlike some so-called success stories in the corporate world, the people involved in this miracle were not a handpicked group of superstars. Instead, the Elizabethtown plant achieved its dramatic results using the same group of employees and managers who worked there *during its worst years*. This proves beyond any doubt that in the proper environment of commitment, training, and support, people can change, grow, and prosper.

Through the years, we have witnessed many such examples of organizations that made the commitment to change and did what was needed to see the transformation through to completion. All started with a new vision and then moved swiftly into the process of identifying strengths and weaknesses. This process is crucial, as we will see in the next chapter.

CHAPTER 11

Assessing Strengths
and Weaknesses

I f you want to take a trip, there are two fundamental questions
that must be answered. The first is easy: *Where do you want to
go?* The second may seem obvious, but it must be asked nonethe-
less: *What is your starting point?*

Without this second piece of data, your chances for a successful journey drop to zero. It is virtually impossible to make travel
plans without knowing both your destination *and* your point of departure. If you want to visit Sydney, Australia, the route you take,
the cost, and the timetable will all be determined by where you
begin. For example, if you start your excursion from a suburb of
Sydney, you will likely use an automobile as your mode of trans-
portation, the cost will be several dollars' worth of gasoline, and
the entire trip will take just a matter of minutes. If your journey
begins in Los Angeles, California, however, you will have to take
an airplane instead of a car to get there, it will take approximately
fourteen hours from takeoff to landing, and it will certainly cost
more. The route that you take is determined by where your journey begins, not ends.

This principle is just as true when it comes to organizational
change. In the past decade or so, leaders have realized the sig-

nificant role played by statements of vision, mission, and values in identifying the desired end for their organizations. In other words, they have become more intentional about their destinations. Yet, amazingly, many of these same leaders refuse to invest what is necessary to clearly understand their points of departure. Whenever this happens the results are always the same: confusion, frustration, and time wasted wandering in circles.

> YOUR ROUTE IS DETERMINED BY WHERE YOUR JOURNEY BEGINS, NOT ENDS.

Years ago my grandfather taught me the importance of this concept as we hunted and fished together in the forests of northern Michigan. He explained in simple terms that survival in the woods is a matter of three fundamental issues. First, never panic, no matter how scary the situation looks. Second, make sure you have a survival kit so you are prepared for emergencies. Third, always have a sense of where you are. Despite my grandfather's advice, there have been times that I have wandered for hours before finally returning to camp. In those times of directional impairment—OK, I admit that I was lost—it has been crystal clear that the real issue is not where I want to go. That's the easy part; obviously I want to go back to camp. Instead, the matter of paramount importance is simply this: *Where am I now?* Have I wandered too far to the north, south, east, or west? Am I just a few degrees off of my intended course, or am I completely turned around?

These same questions should be asked by organizational leaders before they attempt to go anywhere. Often they are not, and that is a good way to get lost.

The Three General Starting Points

At any moment in time, an organization's fundamental condition or starting point can be classified in one of three ways: ideal, acceptable, or unacceptable. The *ideal* condition means that there is no need for any change or improvement. This is a rare situation, but it can happen. *Acceptable* means that critical issues are under control; some competitive opportunities exist, however, and there is room for change. Finally, *unacceptable* means that the mission is in jeopardy from one or more critical issues, and change is needed immediately.

All leaders should take time to honestly determine which of these terms best describes the overall condition of their organization. If the organization is in its *ideal* state, then obviously its leadership has done a fantastic job of pursing the mission, living the values, and serving its customers. If, however, the organization is in either the *acceptable* or *unacceptable* state, then competitive opportunities exist and should be pursued. The challenge is deciding exactly which route to take.

Which Way Should We Go?

Every year millions of dollars and hundreds of thousands of hours are wasted as leaders of organizations worldwide race for a prize called excellence without ever reaching the finish line. A primary reason for this is the lack of honest assessment of the organization's strengths and weaknesses, especially in the area of human relations. The concepts of assessment and evaluation are certainly not foreign to most organizations. In fact, it is common for leaders to evaluate some parts of their company on a regular basis. Many businesses perform detailed audits of their finances and physical inventory every three to six months. Few would challenge the wisdom of such practices. However, if it makes sense to assess these indicators of organizational health, then does it not also make sense to evaluate the overall condition of human relations?

It is especially important to determine levels of employee morale, the quality of interpersonal relationships, and the degree of leadership effectiveness throughout the organization. Sadly, these issues are often neglected, resulting in serious consequences for both the culture and bottom-line performance. It is crucial to remember that every change in an organization affects its people and, perhaps more importantly, its people affect every change. Employees, volunteers, and others involved either promote or resist change, depending on their level of commitment to the process. In addition, their commitment to the process is largely determined by their relationships with others in their organization, especially their leaders.

I recall some research from several years ago that showed the power of the relationship between organizational leaders and followers. The study showed that when union leaders attempted to organize workers in various industries, the number one issue that determined whether employees voted for or against joining the union was not wages, benefits, or overall working conditions. Instead, it was the quality of the relationship that the employees had with their first-line supervisors. Surprising? It shouldn't be. We all have an inherent need to feel secure, respected, and valued by others. Supervisors and managers who fail to lead others with kindness, civility, and professionalism literally force employees to look for other institutions, such as unions, to satisfy these basic needs. The solution to this begins with awareness. Too many managers, administrators, and business owners know minute details about their company's inventory levels, up to the exact returns on investment and complex production schedules, yet are oblivious to the condition of human relations within their organizations.

> EVERY ORGANIZATIONAL CHANGE AFFECTS PEOPLE . . . AND PEOPLE AFFECT EVERY CHANGE.

The Need for Assessment

Not long ago, a lesson about the need for ongoing organization assessment was brought home to me in an unusual way. I had just finished teaching a leadership seminar and a young manager approached me. I was shocked by the expression on his face as he approached me after the session. Tears on his cheeks were the outward expression of the pain inside. Something I said about relationships had obviously brought his pent-up emotions to the surface. During the bittersweet conversation that followed he slowly explained that his world had recently collapsed when, after eight years of marriage, his wife decided to leave him.

A worn photograph from his wallet spoke volumes about their lives together. In it were my new friend, his wife, and their son and daughter. In the background stood the family home, two late-model cars, and a newly constructed swimming pool. I complimented him on his beautiful family, and then, to try to cheer him, I mentioned his impressive house. His response proved that he had truly learned a lot in recent months. "The house is a monument to my stupidity," he quietly lamented. "I built it by working every hour of overtime I possibly could. I was never home. Even on the weekends I worked a second job until late at night. At first we were so happy there, but soon the excitement wore off. My wife asked me to cut back on some of the overtime and make some changes, but I didn't listen. I just kept working . . . and now she is gone. Man, I never saw it coming."

My heart ached as this young man carefully put his memories back into his wallet and walked toward the door. I pondered what he had shared with me. What had he done wrong to cause his family to disintegrate? Was his big mistake that he worked too much overtime? Not exactly. As I saw it then and still see it today, he never took time to assess where he was, where he was going, and—most importantly—to ask the other members of his "organization" what they thought.

Assessment Options

An organizational assessment may be approached in various ways, each having its own pluses and minuses. For instance, data may be gathered by either internal or external personnel. Also, it may be collected from the entire organization or from a much smaller sample. Finally, the assessment may be designed to utilize objective, numerical data from a computerized survey, or it may be based upon more subjective data gathered through face-to-face interviews, or it may utilize a combination of both.

While multiple options exist for its design, the threefold purpose of an assessment remains constant. The first purpose is to obtain accurate perceptions of the strengths and weaknesses of the organization from people at all levels. The second purpose is to gather, compile, and report the assessment results in a way that leaders can understand and act upon them. The final purpose is to involve all members of the organization in the process of change. With that in mind, let's compare the various approaches to see which are preferable.

Limited Surveys Using Internal Personnel

Assessment surveys completed by management staff or other employees may be easy to schedule and will generally be completed at a fairly low cost. There are two significant drawbacks to this approach, however. First, the in-house personnel may not have the credibility with employees needed to succeed. In addition, workers may not trust the interviewer to remain impartial when confronted with criticism of the organization. The ultimate problem with interviewers who are not professionals in this field is that they can easily miss critical cues from the people being questioned. I have learned, over the years, that what employees are *not* willing to discuss is just as important as what they are willing to share during an assessment interview. It makes me very nervous, therefore, to have a novice attempt to assess an organization's human relations climate.

The assessment process is much more difficult than it may appear, and a human relations assessment is much more complex than other standard inventory procedures in the corporate world. Counting parts is much easier than looking into hearts. A professional assessor is doing much more than just numbering cans on a shelf. Indeed, he or she is probing the uncharted depths of human thought, emotion, and commitment. If an organization has the ability to invest the time and financial resources, it is therefore always best to have an impartial professional perform the assessment.

There are some exceptions to this. For example, in relatively small, cohesive groups, such as a family, one of the leaders—in this case, a parent—may simply call a meeting to discuss each member's perception of the family's state of wellness. It is also possible for small, closely held businesses to be assessed in this manner. However, in families, businesses, churches, or other organizations where there is strife, mistrust, and/or unresolved conflict, it is better to have someone from the outside assist with the information gathering. In large organizations the in-house approach simply will not work. To be effective in this environment the assessors not only must be credible, competent, and unbiased, but also must be *perceived* to have these qualities by the people to be interviewed.

Full Assessment Using an External Professional

The reasons for utilization of an external professional are many. They include high credibility, a track record of successfully evaluating other organizations, the lack of mistrust by employees, perception of impartiality, and more. The downside of this approach is that it can take more time to schedule the interviews and there is a cost for the service.

Through the years, my associates and I have interviewed many thousands of people using a systematic approach that gathers information from nearly 100 percent of an organization's members. This approach is time-consuming and tedious, but it is the most effective way to obtain a complete picture of what is happening inside an organization. It is like a doctor who is attempting to diagnose a patient with internal problems. If the doctor is wise, he or she will not be satisfied simply to look at the outside of the patient and then recommend treatment. Instead, x-rays, CAT scans, and other advanced methods of determining what is actually happening *inside* the patient will be ordered. A proper diagnosis generally results in a healthy patient; conversely, a casual, skin-deep diagnosis may cause the patient to suffer or even die. So it is with an organizational assessment. You must look below the surface, into the depths of the organization, to truly understand its strengths and weaknesses.

I am convinced that this type of "x-ray" assessment is best achieved when face-to-face interviews are conducted with the vast majority of the people involved. For this reason, I am strongly ly opposed to computerized surveys that attempt to gather input from a so-called "representative sample" of people. The upside of this method is speed. However, the downside is formidable. With all due respect to the world's statisticians, I believe this is a very dangerous method of determining what employees are really thinking. People differ from department to department and from one work shift to another, which means that the notion of a "representative sample" is a myth.

> A COMPLETE ASSESSMENT PROVIDES A CLEAR AND CRITICAL X-RAY OF ORGANIZATIONAL TRUTHS.

The Blind Men and the Elephant

It is much like the story of the blind men who attempted to describe an elephant by touching it in various spots. One man touched the elephant's side and described it as a wall. Another touched its trunk and described it as a snake. Still another man touched the elephant's leg and described it as a tree. Each was firmly convinced that he had a complete understanding about elephants. What these men really needed was someone from outside their group to help combine all of their perceptions. Then, and only then, they would have a detailed picture of what an elephant really looks like.

I have seen this story played out countless times in the corporate world by modern-day blind men. These people honestly believe that they have grasped the cause of their organization's problems, when in fact they see only a small part of it. One individual brings a defective part into a manufacturing meeting and declares that a lack of quality is the problem. Another brings in a report about a customer complaint and is certain that customer service is where to invest the company's resources. Still another overhears two employees arguing in the hallway and states emphatically that the organization's problem is a lack of teamwork.

The impact of these different perceptions can be profound. Why? Because the way you define a problem dictates how you solve it. The organization may invest hundreds of thousands of dollars into a program to "fix" product quality, customer service, or broken relationships without ever confirming that these approaches are needed to solve the actual problems. Further, if the organization has limited resources to invest into any of these efforts, then the program that has the backing of the highest-ranking manager or the most convincing orator will end up with the funds. A careful assessment will reveal the entire picture and provide direction for the future.

The Hidden Benefits of an Assessment

There is more to a properly performed assessment than just gathering data about an organization. I have found that assessments not only uncover the real strengths and weaknesses of an organization but also can unify and prepare people for change. I believe that at least 50 percent of the value gained from an assessment comes from the fact that each person involved develops ownership in the change process. They know that their input will be used to move the organization in a new direction, and they want to help shape their own collective destiny.

It is important to remember two things about assessments: first, people feel ownership for things that they help to build. Second, people take care of what they own. Meaningful involvement in an assessment, therefore, increases the sense of ownership in the organizational change process. For this reason, it is wise to involve as many people as possible in an assessment.

Assessment Topics

The following is a list of topics we typically use to assess business, government, health care, unions, and religious organizations. They are some of the universal causes for relational breakdown and low organizational effectiveness.

Mission

What is the mission of the organization?

Critical Issues and Competitive Opportunities

What are the critical issues and competitive opportunities that need to be addressed in order to achieve the mission?

Core Values and Operating Principles

What are the core values of the organization? Are the core values and operating principles adhered to consistently?

Trust and Openness

What is the current level of trust and openness within the organization? Are leaders credible? Has sufficient time been spent developing relationships that foster trust?

Leader Effectiveness

How productive is the organization? Is the mission being accomplished? Are followers motivated or demotivated by their interaction with leaders?

Communication and Listening Skills

How effective is the communication process within the organization? When people speak, do they achieve complete understanding and build positive relationships? Is vital information lost during the communication process?

Information Flow

Does the organization have methods and systems in place to keep people properly informed? Are leaders aware of their followers' concerns, problems, and suggestions? Are followers informed of critical issues, updates, challenges, and successes that the organization has experienced?

Interdependence

Do people recognize that they need each other to achieve the mission? Do members of the organization understand how other levels, areas, and individuals actually function and how their work relates to the mission?

Morale

What is the current level of morale? Does it differ from area to area? Are leaders motivated, encouraged, energized, and committed to the mission? Is the morale of followers different than that of leaders? If so, why?

Positive Reinforcement

How do people know when they have performed well? Is acceptable and ideal performance recognized? In what ways is it recognized? Is there a formal or informal method of rewarding people? If so, is it consistent?

Corrective Feedback

How do people know when they have performed poorly? Is unacceptable performance recognized and corrected? Is assistance given when someone cannot perform to the agreed-upon standards? Is discipline administered fairly and equally?

Performance Enhancement Process

Is there a formal system in place to develop the skills of personnel in the organization? How is it administered? Are training, coaching, and counseling available to those who want or need it?

Approach to Problem Solving

How are problems addressed? Do a few high-level people try to solve the majority of the problems and make most of the decisions for the organization? Is a systematic approach used to address problems? Have all members of the organization been trained in problem solving?

A Word to the Wise

An organizational assessment is often like cleaning out a teenager's closet—you never know what you will discover. You may find some hidden treasures as well as things that are not very pleasant. Assessments often pinpoint a certain manager or supervisor who is having a negative impact on his or her followers. It is vital in these instances to remember that an assessment is not intended as an individual performance review, but rather is designed to identify positive and negative trends within the organization.

The Final Steps

Once the assessment interviews are complete, there are still two very important steps that must be completed. First, the results must be presented to the appropriate people. Naturally this includes the leaders who commissioned the survey; but it also includes all others who invested time and emotional energy into the process. This step is often left out, resulting in reduced credibility for the leaders and even lower morale for the followers.

The last step in the assessment process is for the appropriate leaders to utilize the assessment data as the foundation for the development of a long-term strategic plan. Occasionally leaders ask for input from others and then fail to act upon the information given. This is one of the quickest ways for leaders to lose the commitment of their followers. For an assessment to have the desired results the leaders who requested the information must follow a simple three-step process: ask, think, act. Ask for the input, think about its relevance for organizational success, and then act upon the critical issues and competitive opportunities that the assessment reveals.

> AN ORGANIZATIONAL ASSESSMENT IS LIKE CLEANING OUT A TEENAGER'S CLOSET— YOU NEVER KNOW WHAT YOU WILL FIND.

CHAPTER 12

The Good, the Bad, and the Ugly: Responding to Assessment Data

"This is terrible!" moaned the myopic manager. "We can't let the employees hear these assessment results. There are too many problems! What will they think?"

This was one general manager's initial response to the results of his organization's assessment. Until then the assessment process had gone according to plan. In our initial meetings this gentleman said all of the right things about wanting to change the company's operation to achieve excellence. The memo he sent prior to the assessment interviews urged employees at all levels to be completely honest with their thoughts about the company. During the interviews, employees seemed genuinely pleased to have the opportunity to identify the strengths and weaknesses of their organization. My team and I finished our final interviews right on schedule and were satisfied that we had captured the basis for solid recommendations for change.

After the interviews we flew home and spent several days

compiling and analyzing the assessment data. The report was typical of what we find in many of today's companies: many strengths along with some concerns about poor communication and overly autocratic management practices. Soon our report was complete and I returned to communicate the findings, first to the general manager and his immediate staff, then to the rest of the employees. I expected the leaders to receive the feedback with some concern and then move quickly to the creation of an improvement plan. I was wrong.

As I shared the assessment results with the top leader and his staff, I soon learned just how wrong my expectations were. Despite the fact that virtually every deficiency in the report could be addressed, the general manager became increasingly frantic. The fact that his employees viewed the organization as less than perfect sent this normally unflappable man into an irrational panic.

> THE STILLNESS WAS BROKEN WHEN THE MANAGER MUMBLED AGAIN, "WHAT WILL THEY THINK?"

He seemed petrified at the thought of presenting the results to his three hundred employees who were assembling—at that moment—in the company's cramped meeting room down the hall. (Normally, organizational leaders take several days for reflection before having us share the information with their employees. In this instance, the leaders insisted that we do it in rapid succession. I suppose it seemed like a good idea at the time!)

Now it was my turn to panic at the thought of not presenting the results to the employees, since I had promised during the survey interviews that they would hear the same report as their managers. After this poor man's third outburst, we all sat in painful silence, wondering what to do. The stillness was broken when the top manager mumbled again, "What will they think?"

This happened nearly two decades ago, but I still vividly remember the turmoil of the day. Composing myself, I gave him a response that was short, but not sweet. I told him that the employees would *think* three things. First, since the data that he was now so afraid of came from them, they would *think* that we accurately recorded what they said during the interviews. Second, they would *think* that he, their leader, actually cared enough to commission the assessment and then listen to their concerns. Third, they would *think* that the problems that the employees have known about all along were finally going to be addressed.

After a great deal of persuasion, the general manager was finally convinced that his employees wouldn't be shocked, discouraged, or quit because of the company's problems—especially since they were the ones who identified them in the first place. That was progress. We eventually made our way to the meeting room and I began to present the assessment results. I couldn't help but notice the poor general manager's pained expression each time I talked about a problem area. Predictably, the reaction of the employees was quite the opposite. They neither winced nor gloated over their company's

> ON HIS FACE WAS THE LOOK OF SOMEONE WHO HAD TAKEN TOO MANY ROLLER COASTER RIDES.

shortcomings. Instead, they sat quietly and occasionally nodded in agreement until the final issues were shared.

At the conclusion of the feedback session, one employee stood and addressed the red-faced manager, who braced himself, expecting the worst. His fears were unfounded. The employee explained that he and his coworkers were glad to know that management was finally going to address some of the long-term problems. Then he simply thanked the general manager and his staff for commissioning the assessment, pledged his support for the effort, and sat down. As the employees left the room, many of them came to the manager and voiced their support for the process as well. When the room was finally empty, the manger sat in silence for several minutes. On his face was the look of someone who had taken one too many rides on a roller coaster.

We eventually moved forward and provided some training for his employees, but this project never came close to reaching its full potential. The reason was quite simple. Even after the feedback session, this manager spent more time trying to justify the shortcomings of his organization than fixing them. Fortunately, this type of response to an assessment is not the norm. While it is very common for most top managers, government officials, administrators, pastors, or parents to feel some disappointment when negative results are revealed, most want to move quickly into the next phase: building on the strengths and addressing the weaknesses.

The Need to Know

Over the years, I have witnessed a full range of reactions, from laughter to tears, to assessment reports. While responses vary, one thing remains constant: the importance of knowing the truth about one's organization. Plans for success must be founded upon facts—not rumors, assumptions, guesses, or even what proved to be true in someone else's company. A properly performed assessment reveals truth that, in turn, provides the foundation for an organization's plan for change.

Today, plant managers, pastors, and parents all have significantly different roles than those of their predecessors. As a result of the rapidly changing world around them, these leaders must now be masters of multitasking. Within each leader's ever-expanding job description there is often little time to analyze, comprehend, and respond to what is happening within the workplace or within the home. These dedicated leaders don't know what they don't know, and those around them will not automatically keep them informed. In this environment leaders often remain blissfully—or stressfully—unaware of major problems until they explode. In business, government, ministry, and parenting, having the correct information upon which to plan is the key to victory. Hard work is not enough. Dedication is not enough. The Light Brigade of the British cavalry had both, and look what happened to them.

We can never reach our potential without understanding our organization's strengths and weaknesses. A thorough assessment provides this information and should be conducted in each organization every one to two years.

Perception Is Reality

Assessment information should always be compiled in a document that is then carefully studied by organizational leaders before any plans for change are made. It takes time to understand the various perceptions that people have about the organization. Knowing this, leaders must fight against the tendency to offer rebuttals or to discount the input of their employees. Organizational assessments are not conducted as witch hunts or to place blame on individuals whose performance is not exemplary. Instead, they are intended to provide insights into the strengths and opportunities for enhanced competitiveness as perceived by all members of the organization.

Leaders who examine the assessment information should remember one foundational truth: *perception is reality*. In other words, some of the information contained in the assessment may not be *true*, even though it is *real* to the person who shared it with the assessor. For example, I have often heard foundational-level employees describe their leaders as uncaring and unsympathetic. In these instances, the workers are firmly convinced that their perceptions are accurate and they act upon their beliefs in a host of negative manners. Subsequent discussions with the supposed cold-hearted managers, however, reveal that they really did care about their employees. Unfortunately, up until that point the leaders had not demonstrated that which was in their hearts, thereby creating the negative perceptions. Once the assessment proved that this was the case, the managers were able to change their behaviors and communication patterns to align their actions with their values.

Feedback to Everyone

Soon after the assessment information has been compiled and reviewed by those in leadership, the results should be communicated to everyone who participated in the interviews. This is contrary to the practice of many organizations that conduct opinion surveys with no feedback mechanism to employees. The feedback is essential for building the trust that is needed for change throughout the organization.

Leaders, like the manager I mentioned at the beginning of this chapter, often resist sharing negative information for fear that it will show weaknesses in the organization or its leadership. This is faulty thinking for two reasons. First, employees are well aware of the organization's deficiencies and are glad that leaders are finally going to address the problems. Openness with the results is seen as a sign of strength and integrity rather than as weakness. Second, commitment from all levels within the organization is vital; and sharing the assessment results allows everyone to participate fully in the change process, thus promoting commitment. For these reasons, the feedback should go first to the organization's leaders and then, after they have had time to process it, to all others who contributed to the survey.

Feedback Methods and Lessons Learned

Not only should the information gathered during an assessment be reported to everyone who participated in the interviews, it should be done in person—not through memos or bulletins, which are often misinterpreted. Once an assessment or survey has been commissioned, leaders should always share the results with followers and allow sufficient time for questions and answers.

There are some simple guidelines to follow during this process. First, leaders shouldn't promise that all problems will be solved within a short period. That is unrealistic. Followers simply need to hear that the issues will be dealt with in a reasonable amount of time. In addition, leaders shouldn't minimize, place blame (except upon themselves if appropriate), or make excuses for any shortcomings exposed in the assessment. Excuses are not reasons. Excuses do not create positive change, only plans of action do.

Finally, leaders should be prepared to explain the inevitable misunderstandings that the assessment identifies. In my experience, from 20 to 40 percent of the problems identified during an assessment are actually a result of misperception, miscommunication, and misunderstanding. These are easily reconciled with proper explanation, which gives an immediate morale boost to the organization.

A Word of Caution

Again, unlike the misguided manager mentioned earlier, leaders *must* accept the survey results with an open mind. If the data is critical of the organization or its leadership, resentment too often is the primary reaction. Leaders must understand that the employees did not identify problems to hurt anyone's feelings; they did so to help the organization become its best. An immature response from leaders can do real damage to their credibility, so it must be avoided.

The tendency to reject critical or negative assessment data has been going on for decades. My father spent thirty years as a high-level manager in one of America's largest automotive manufacturing companies. His organization often conducted surveys to measure progress, performance, and employee opinions. One such survey found fault with top management, identified numerous areas for improvement, and criticized the overall lack of purpose and direction. My dad and his peers were amazed, amused, and ultimately disturbed by their general manager's response to the survey. Rather than address the deficiencies, he angrily concluded that the company that had conducted the survey was incompetent and immediately commissioned a new survey. That was the beginning of the end of his credibility. Predictably, the next survey produced essentially the same results. Even more predictably, the executive refused to accept it as well—and that *was* the end of his credibility.

Remember, the goal of an assessment is to determine what problems exist and how to address them, not to point blame at who may or may not have caused the problems. A proper assessment is designed to focus on future change, not on past blame. Approached in this positive manner, the organization is now ready to move forward into a brighter future.

The Blueprint for Change

Once an assessment has been completed and accepted by leadership, things begin to get exciting! The assessment has identified the organization's strengths and weaknesses. Even if serious weaknesses in relationships, communication, or other areas are found, leaders are motivated and mobilized because they now know where to focus their energies. Leaders may spend additional time studying the document and investigating all employee concerns, past and present. This quick look back at the history of the organization often clears up years of resentment and insures that mistakes do not recur.

After careful study, top leaders prepare their responses to the assessment report and then share both the response and the original report with all members of the organization. The initial reaction ranges from skepticism to euphoria. Finally the truth is known about their organization. This sets the minds of employees free as a vision of a better future comes into view. Leaders have clarified the mission, core values, priorities, and operating principles. The stage is set for success.

You *Can* Get There from Here

Once the organizational assessment has been completed, the time of aimless wandering is over. This newly acquired information, coupled with the vision, mission, core values, and operating principles, points the way to the ultimate destination—success. To arrive there with a minimum of wasted time and backtracking, organizational leaders now must develop a comprehensive blueprint for strategic development. It is time to release the power of a plan.

PART THREE

Purpose and Direction

CHAPTER 13

The Power of a Plan

S uccessful organizations invest considerable time in planning for peak performance in a variety of areas, including information systems, marketing, facility utilization, equipment, product innovation, quality assurance, profitability, and productivity. Sadly, the human or cultural side of the planning process is often overlooked or viewed as less important than these other issues. This is tunnel vision of the worst kind. Why? Because the people involved are integrally involved with these other issues. They will create the product innovations, build in the quality, increase profits, and more. A proper strategic plan always includes the human side of the organizational equation. Without one, there will be no win/win/win.

Some of the most common cultural issues included in a strategic plan are leadership effectiveness, teamwork, communications, technical skills, and customer service. An inventory of behaviors needed is created and then plans are made to insure that the people involved have the skills and abilities to demonstrate them. The plan may include training, coaching, counseling, on-the-job training, job shadowing, and more.

Culture by Design

The following is an example of a strategic plan for cultural change that we helped a recent client create.

The process began when the organization's leaders revisited their statements of vision, mission, and core values to affirm the type of culture that they wanted to create. (We will explore the concepts of vision, mission, and values in following chapters.) Next, they conducted an extensive organizational assessment that showed the strengths and weaknesses of that organization. The assessment data was analyzed to determine which issues posed the greatest threat to the mission and which issues held the greatest competitive opportunities.

The leaders then designed a comprehensive strategic plan to help all employees contribute to the mission and demonstrate the values on a daily basis. As the plan was formulated, we made sure that each component addressed and fulfilled some aspect of the mission, core values, or operating principles.

We then wrote the following statement of intent as the foundation for the strategic plan. This statement helped keep the group on track and served to introduce the overall developmental initiative to the rest of the organization. The statement was further expanded by adding some specific goals. All are reprinted below.

Statement of Intent for the Strategic Plan

Our cultural development plan is designed to deliver a comprehensive process that includes:

- Cultural awareness and alignment
- Clear behavioral expectations
- Leadership and staff development
- Customer service enhancements

- Process improvement
- Effective change management

Goals for the Implementation of the Strategic Plan

- *Cultural Transformation:* We intend to focus on the adaptations necessary to maintain an aligned culture and to respond effectively to a changing environment.

- *Education and Professional Development:* We intend to promote competence and character in all leaders and staff, encouraging effective performance and continuous improvement.

- *Systems and Work Processes:* We intend to focus on standards, evaluation, and continuous process improvements, using team problem solving and creativity to promote effective systems.

The information above provided a broad framework for our plan. Next, it was time to identify a list of projects needed to achieve the goals and carry out the plan.

Based on the company's mission and values statements and our assessment data, we selected the following projects to pursue. We developed specific education and training activities for each project to insure that the people involved had the skills and information needed for success.

Cultural Development Projects

- Cultural orientation meetings for all current employees
- New employee orientation sessions
- New manager/supervisor orientation sessions
- Internal communications audit and enhancement process
- Annual employee survey and follow-up

Leadership Development Projects

- Coaching and mentoring process
- Leadership-training courses
- Team building for executive team and management group
- Continuous reinforcement activities

Staff Development Projects

- Interpersonal relationships training
- Team building and targeted intervention where needed
- Quality and customer service initiatives
- Customer service team and network development
- Facilitation and team leader training
- Problem-solving and decision-making training
- Continuous quality improvement training

Once we identified the major projects and specific activities needed to build the desired corporate culture, all that remained was to create a long-term schedule or calendar of events. This was very tedious due to the complexities of scheduling large numbers of people. However, investing several hours on this task during the initial planning saved many days that would have been wasted later.

The final part of the strategic planning process was to decide which activities would be scheduled first. As in most strategic plan implementations, we began with leadership development so that the organization's executives and managers were prepared to model the proper behaviors of the new culture. Once we selected leadership training as the initial undertaking, we then decided on the details of the training content, the training schedule, the number of training days, and which leaders would attend first.

After the training began, we identified the logical next project and repeated the scheduling process until all activities were on the calendar. In later chapters, we will explore specific training content and educational topics that are typically presented to both leaders and followers.

Momentum for Change

Once the strategic plan for cultural development is created, it is pursued in combination with the organization's statement of mission, core values, and operating principles. At this stage, the change initiative is like a giant rock that is beginning to roll downhill. It may have been difficult to move initially, but now it is virtually impossible to stop. The people involved know the organization's purpose and direction and understand the strategic plan that is being implemented. Armed with the new skills learned in training, they are not only willing but are now more than able to make it happen. This process works in small organizations, large organizations, and even in entire communities, as we will explore in the next chapter.

CHAPTER 14

A New Vision

"Everything that can be invented
has been invented."

—*Charles Duell, Commissioner,*
United States Office of Patents, 1899

M r. Duell was obviously more than a bit shortsighted in his prediction made so many years ago. Inventions continue to happen by the thousands. Each begins as a "vision." The process for invention and innovation is constant. Someone sees something that no one else has seen and then successfully brings that vision into being. With all of the problems, challenges, and opportunities in the world, I am certain that people will continue to invent things until the end of time. Regardless of whether the invention is a new vaccine for cancer, better toothpaste, or the next billion-dollar dot-com company, it will all begin with a new vision.

The myriad of opportunities, however, does not make the process of realizing a new vision any easier. I suppose that in a perfect world we would wake up one morning with a divinely inspired vision to create a new organization to make life better for all of humanity. Then, shortly after our first cup of coffee, we would transform that vision into a compelling statement of mission for others to follow. By midmorning we would simply set our goals, gather committed followers around us, and assign projects and tasks. And by nightfall our vision would be realized. Unfortunately, the world we live in is far from perfect; so plans never come together that easily.

New Vision = Hard Work

The concept of vision is not for the faint of heart or for those who tremble at the thought of change. People who live life by the now-famous phrase, "If it isn't broken, don't try to fix it," as their motto will always struggle with vision. Why? Because in order to embrace a new vision, one must let go of the old. The resulting change in the status quo forces everyone involved to leave the comfort zones in which they live or work.

In an organizational setting, such as a business, ministry, or hospital, it is impossible to implement a new vision unless the leaders become aware of the need for change. This may sound overly simple, but in my experience many leaders simply do not realize that their nations, businesses, or families are in desperate need of change until it is too late. These people fly through life blinded by the pace or complexity of it all until something happens to shock them into reality.

This awareness of the need to change may come from a variety of positive experiences, such as reading books, attending conferences, or talking with others who are changing their own organizations. However, awareness of the need to make significant adjustments also comes from extremely negative experiences as well. Employees go on strike, customers take their business elsewhere, spouses demand divorce, and children run away from home. Too often the leaders involved are caught off-guard by the crises that seemingly came out of nowhere. It is infinitely better for us to look continually at ways to make things better around us.

Vision Basics

The concept of vision within the organizational setting is applied in two distinct ways. First, a *creative vision* is needed to bring a new organization into existence. Second, a new vision may come at a time when an existing organization is functioning and either struggling to succeed or when its leaders are aware that they have the potential to perform at a completely new level. This is called a *transformational vision*. Let's look at each one in more detail.

A Creative Vision

A creative vision occurs at the exact instant a new idea springs to life. Just as in the marvelous process of procreation, there is a precise moment when something that has never been before comes into existence. The uniqueness of every human being on earth bears testimony to the power of creation. In like manner, every organization on earth today started as a vision in someone's mind and grew from

> ALL GREAT INVENTIONS WERE BORN FROM A CREATIVE VISION.

there. The great inventions of history, such as the wheel, electricity, and room service, are all innovations born from a creative vision.

Another powerful example of this concept comes from the 1960s, when American president John F. Kennedy shared a compelling vision for the United States' space program: putting a man on the moon. In today's world we scarcely think about the fact that scores of humans have flown into space, spent time living in orbiting space stations, and flown back to the earth, landing at the place of their choosing. This was certainly not the case when Mr. Kennedy shocked the world with his novel idea of manned space travel.

The reaction at the time was predictable: "Send a man to the moon? Moreover, get him back safely? Impossible!" Fortunately, the president surrounded himself with people who had faith in his dream, and the work began. Since nothing like that had ever been done before, naturally there was no existing plan to modify, change, or revise. Kennedy's amazing project, and the organization to support it, had to be grown from conception to maturity. The vision became real when, in 1969, Neil Armstrong made history by being the first human to walk on the surface of the moon and uttered the now-famous words, "One small step for man, one giant leap for mankind."

A Transformational Vision

The second application where vision is utilized in the organizational setting occurs when significant change is needed. This vision often springs forth when someone in authority realizes that his or her organization has entered into a sort of midlife crisis and, without changes, risks premature disability or death. Instead of high blood pressure, fatigue, and weight problems, the warning signs relate to the organization's productivity, quality, sales, attendance numbers, and so on. Faced with this reality, the leaders must choose either to accept their fate and prepare for the worst or to redesign, reengineer, and revitalize their organization so that it can drive energetically into the future. Under these circumstances, the organization needs to be completely transformed if it is to succeed.

Another word to describe this process is *revitalization*. While not many people actually invent something new during their lifetimes, we all have opportunities to make our business, ministry, community, family, or personal life better through a process of revitalization. A quick study of the word itself puts us on the right track. *Re* means to return or to revisit something. *Vitalize* springs from the root word *vita*, meaning "life." Combined, this word compels us to return to the original purpose of our organization and to put new life into it. It is never too late to revitalize any aspect of our personal or professional lives.

Over the years, I have worked with many organizations that had quietly drifted from their original moorings and needed to be brought safely back to port. Others had become stagnant for a variety of reasons and actually needed to launch out in a new direction. So many companies and ministries today are learning that yesterday's performance is no longer good enough to secure tomorrow's future. I have also encountered some very extreme situations, wherein the leaders had concluded that their companies were nearing the end of the corporate lifecycle and without a new vision, enhanced performance, and some very dramatic changes, death was imminent.

During these times of intense organizational soul-searching, it is important for leaders to study the organization's original vision, mission, and values and then compare them to what is currently happening. Have they strayed from the original path? Alternatively, has the original path become impassable due to changing conditions? The answers to these questions help show the way forward. A wise man, George Santayana, once said, "Those who cannot remember the past are condemned to repeat it." He is speaking about negative aspects of the past, which, if forgotten, will often be repeated. A thorough analysis of past, present, and future helps insure that mistakes will be avoided and opportunities seized as the new vision is created.

Vision to Be the Best

A transformational vision may also be cast when an organization is in the prime of life. Watchful leaders often realize the existence of significant opportunities for growth, improvement, and/or competitive advantage even during times of peak performance. We see examples of this transformational mindset in the world of athletics, where world-class competitors continually strive to raise their levels of performance. Runners with years of experience and countless trophies still look for ways to outdistance the competition. To do so they employ innovative approaches to strength training, increased intervals, and enhanced nutrition.

Pioneering leaders around the world use the transformational process to introduce new product lines, build new strategic alliances, and expand existing services into uncharted territory. Enterprising religious leaders have found new ways to entice parishioners to spend time in fellowship with each other by installing high-tech coffee bars in their lobbies. There is no shortage of opportunities for transformation. All it takes is vision.

> INNOVATIVE LEADERS USE THE TRANSFORMATIONAL PROCESS TO INTRODUCE NEW PRODUCT LINES, BUILD NEW ALLIANCES, AND EXPAND INTO UNCHARTED TERRITORIES.

It makes great strategic sense for all leaders to pause regularly and ponder their organization's past, present, and future. Billionaire Bill Gates, the founder of Microsoft, was once asked if he felt that Microsoft, due to its huge size, could ever be beaten in the marketplace. Mr. Gates' reply speaks volumes: "We wake up every day thinking about companies like Wang, Digital Equipment, or Compaq. They were huge companies that did very well, and they have literally disappeared. . . . We are always saying to ourselves—we have to innovate. We've got to come up with that breakthrough."

Business leaders should regularly ask themselves a few key questions: Are the people here still motivated, happy, and productive? What is the trend of the bottom line? What innovations have been implemented within the organization lately? Likewise, ministry leaders should do an honest assessment of their overall effectiveness by evaluating both internal relationships and external impact. Are people motivated to attend services? Is the ministry having a positive influence within the neighborhood, community, and/or nation in which it resides? What is the evidence of divine favor on the work that is done?

Finally, on a personal level, each of us should regularly challenge ourselves with targeted questions about our health, our priorities, and the quality of relationship with our spouses, children, and others. Leaders who regularly invest time reflecting on these issues will be in a position to take their organization to new heights—even to the moon.

The Visioning Process

As we have seen, a new vision can be created at virtually any stage of life for individuals or organizations. When working on a visioning project with a group such as a board of directors or executive leadership team, I have the members discuss their thoughts and emotions about the proposed vision with each other so that everyone understands not only the words being used but also the rationale and emotion behind them.

All visions are intentionally broad, lofty, and uncluttered by details. They provide an ultimate destination rather than a detailed roadmap for others to follow. For example, the vision for Molitor International was born after a time of some very serious soul-searching during the early 1980s. It took literally weeks to finally sum up what I hoped to achieve, and ultimately I stated it as follows: *I want to see Molitor International become the most effective consulting, coaching, and training firm in the world.*

As stated, this vision is easy to understand and definitely lofty, but it has never provided specific direction to any of our corporate officers, managers, or employees. In addition, while it says something about *what* will be done, it says nothing about *how* it will be done. The purpose of the statement was, is, and always will be simply to focus attention on the ultimate reason for the organization to exist. Based upon this statement, our company will not measure its success by size, money, or market share. Instead, the organization will be measured by its effectiveness in teaching, training, coaching, and helping others achieve their corporate dreams.

One of our larger corporate clients uses a very simple phrase to describe its vision: *To be recognized as our customer's number one supplier.* Some might see this as too plain of a statement to provide much direction, but I believe that it is a near-perfect statement of vision. The phrase clearly focuses on the customer and the company's desire to be first in all categories of importance to that customer. It is not cluttered with details about product lines or geographic locations. It only contains a single element that focuses on the measurement of success: *number one.* That seems clear enough to me.

The Journey . . . Not the Destination

The greatest value of a vision statement comes from the process of getting key leaders together to share, listen, understand, and, finally, agree on the organization's purpose and direction. When completed, the vision process accomplishes one essential task. It brings all of the key decision-makers into agreement on the direction for the organization. Whether parents, top executives, boards of directors, or the elders of a church, these leaders now have a broad target at which to aim not only their efforts but also the efforts of all other members of their organization.

Once the vision is clearly stated, these same leaders must begin to subdivide the vision into component parts so that each person involved completely understands his or her role in the process. The most effective way to accomplish this is to write a detailed statement of mission and utilize that statement as the basis for all subsequent actions.

Some organizations choose to capture their thoughts about vision into a comprehensive vision statement, while others only record their actual statement of mission. Either way, once the vision is created, it provides direction and meaning for all other activities within the organization. We will explore how these concepts work together in following chapters.

A Personal Testimony of the Power of Vision

As any parent can attest, the process of conception is much different than the process of birth. Labor and delivery take time and patience; and, unfortunately, the process produces a great deal of pain. So it is with change initiatives. We can be certain that once a new vision has been conceived much labor will follow. This is where the virtue of commitment is applied. Once a person is convinced that a vision is worth pursuing, he or she should be prepared to sacrifice to see it fulfilled.

When we were expecting our second child, Steven, my wife experienced complications during the pregnancy. Premature labor forced her to remain confined to bed for nearly six months in order to insure that the baby would have time to develop. Kathleen had sporadic contractions during the entire half-year. She was rushed to the hospital no less than five times; and we were in danger of losing our unborn son each time. Through it all Kathleen maintained the vision of a healthy child who would be born if she could endure the difficulty of the pregnancy and the pain of delivery. My wife demonstrated the courage, determination, and patience necessary to see her vision through to completion. She was faithful to the end, and by the grace of God our son was born in perfect health. There is no substitute for commitment in life, and there is nothing to commit to without a vision.

The Transformational Power of Vision

Remember, a vision should be far-reaching and broad in scope. It should stimulate people's imaginations with new possibilities for themselves and their nations, businesses, or families. It should cause them to dream the greatest dream imaginable. Why? Because people today are desperately looking for hope, purpose, and direction for their lives. We need a large enough vision to pull us away from the countless distractions that steal our energy and lull us into complacency—something of greater significance than television, computers, sports, and the pursuit of greater personal wealth. We need visions strong enough to break the power of apathy, fear, and hopelessness in all realms of our society today.

> THE FIRE OF CHANGE IS FUELED BY POSITIVE EXPECTATIONS, AND IT ONLY TAKES A VISION TO LIGHT THE MATCH.

Can just a few well-chosen words really make such a difference? Without question! In drug-ravaged inner cities, individuals with vision are buying and repairing groups of abandoned houses. These homes are then sold to families interested in building productive, crime-free neighborhoods. New businesses are started each day as people with vision discover innovative products and services that can be marketed. Political leaders are beginning to govern based on principles of integrity, fairness, and concern for the well-being of their people. Families are developing new visions for close relationships. The fire of change is fueled by positive expectations, and it takes a vision to light the match. Positive change can happen. Positive change will happen. It only takes a new vision.

What's Your Vision?

There is one additional aspect of vision that should be understood here. That is, an organization should exist in order to bring about a *positive* change in the world—or, more specifically, in a nation, in a community, in families, or in just one individual's life. We must heed the words of genius Albert Einstein, who said, "It has become appallingly obvious that our technology has exceeded our humanity."

The fact that some organizations are formed with the full intent to cause harm to others is very difficult for me to comprehend. Terrorist groups, porn shops, drug lords, polluters, and a wide variety of dishonest businesses do not just appear one day unexpectedly. Rather, someone somewhere actually decided to invest a significant portion of his life to the creation of an organization that will cause death, destruction, humiliation, and/or financial loss to their fellow human beings. These characters can't fathom a win/win/win scenario. Instead, they approach life from an all too common win/lose perspective. How sad.

Each of us should take time to discover if the vision we are pursuing will ultimately benefit others or if it will simply benefit ourselves. The last time I checked, each human being gets approximately eighty years on this earth, during which time we will either make a living honorably, peaceably, and in a manner that benefits others or we will spend our days selfishly devising ways to exploit others. There is precious little middle ground here, so it behooves us to choose wisely. The choice is ours, and it all begins with our vision for life.

CHAPTER 15

The Mission: Clear Purpose and Decisive Direction

Once an organization's vision is clear to its leaders, it must be translated into an achievable mission that others can follow. The importance of this process cannot be overstated. Too often we assume that our employees and others around us understand their roles, responsibilities, and how their efforts contribute to the organization's ultimate success. In many instances this simply is not true. A mission statement guides, justifies, and coordinates all subsequent activities. The power found in a few well-chosen words can be truly astounding. The key, however, is choosing them wisely.

I once worked with an organization that made medical devices used to combat debilitating arthritis in older men and women. This company sought to create a new corporate culture, so we began by having a series of meetings to revisit their original vision and statement of mission. After a short time of discussion, one executive stood up and loudly proclaimed that his company's mission was, as he put it, to "stop pain." He was passionate, persuasive, and extremely shortsighted with his two-word statement of mission. Several other executives tried to move him away from such a statement, but he was adamant. Finally, I asked him if he was sure that he had the most descriptive statement for their organization's mission. Of course he was, he replied. I then proposed two new product lines for their company that would fit perfectly under his statement: narcotics and hit men for hire. The room got very quiet for a few seconds as the team of leaders struggled to find the connection. I offered that if their only mission was to "stop pain," then they could do so by offering customers narcotics and, in the worst-case scenario, have them shot. Bang—no more pain! Soon they understood the absurdity of my suggestion and we were able to move on with a more expansive statement.

Common Sense or Common Practice?

"Common sense": These two simple words are often linked together, but in too many instances they share little in common. An oxymoron at best, this short phrase is often used in hindsight, just after someone does something that was obviously wrong. Nuclear power plants melt down because someone failed to use "common sense." Millions of dollars worth of scrap parts are shipped from factories around the world each year because those involved didn't use "common sense." Thousands of people die in accidents each year because they did things that seemed safe to them at the moment but were recognized by others as a blatant departure from "common sense."

> COMMON SENSE IS MEANINGLESS UNLESS AND UNTIL IT BECOMES COMMON PRACTICE.

In reality, there is no such thing as "common sense," regardless of how often the term is used. For example, why do very few adults place their hands on hot stoves? Because common sense tells them not to, right? Wrong. Adults don't touch hot stoves for one simple reason: at some point in the past they touched one and learned that it was a most unpleasant occurrence. The revelation to avoid hot stoves doesn't come from some innate sense shared by all members of the human family. It comes, instead, from the experience of burned fingers that happened years ago.

The importance of this cannot be overstated for those in organizational leadership. Too many parents, pastors, and company presidents mistakenly believe that all members of their organizations understand where they need to go and the best way to get there. After all, isn't it just common sense? No, of course not—not when people are involved. Common sense is meaningless unless and until it becomes common practice.

Common Mission Leads to Common Sense

Now let's connect the notion of common sense to the concept of mission. Remember that every organization exists for a purpose. That purpose can also be described as its mission. Here is the catch. Organizations are comprised of people, and people have extremely diverse backgrounds due to a lack of commonality in education, training, and life experiences. When a diverse group of people are brought together in an organization such as a bank, hotel, or restaurant, they bring all of those differences with them. This affects how they think, react to stress, solve problems, and interact with customers and coworkers alike. The result is anything but predictable or common. Without an overarching, easy-to-comprehend mission upon which to base their decisions, people will invariably go off in their own direction, creating chaos instead of order.

Mission = Big Picture

Many employees, volunteers, and family members today fail to see the big picture. In other words, they don't understand the specific expectations for them on a daily basis, nor do they understand how their efforts dovetail, complement, and/or potentially conflict with those around them. Several generations ago this was not the case. Artisans worked diligently from start to finish on projects such as rifles, furniture, and wagons, thereby thinking in terms of the whole. This ability to see the big picture was also reinforced by neighbors and families working together on large cooperative projects in which they participated in a project from start to finish, such as building homes and growing crops.

Unfortunately, much of this broad-based understanding has been lost in our modern-day world of assembly lines, office cubicles, and piecemeal work. The more we divide employees and ask them to specialize, the more we need to communicate with them about what is commonly called the "big picture." Failure to do so invariably causes people to shift into compartmentalized thinking that is harmful to the overall mission of their organization. This type of environment causes employees to think and act in extremes. Some believe that their contributions are insignificant and therefore feel like inconsequential specks of dust in the cosmos. At the other end of the spectrum are those who view their work as supremely important and therefore feel as if they are the very center of the universe. Quite a contrast, and yet each position springs from the same well: a failure to properly comprehend the fact that all contributions are significant parts of the whole.

> THE MORE WE ASK EMPLOYEES TO SPECIALIZE, THE MORE THEY NEED TO SEE THE BIG PICTURE.

Important Parts of the Whole

Once employees begin to view themselves and their contributions as being separate from the rest of the organization, they often focus on their own responsibilities with little regard for the needs of others around them. This condition is easy to spot, once you know what to look and listen for. Some of the most obvious indicators of division can be overheard whenever there is a problem. In fact, the voices begin to sound childish, as fingers point and accusations fly. When a problem arises in these settings, you can be sure that the initial communications will center on one issue: *Who is to blame?* Even when there is no significant crisis, the various factions target the others, accusing them of causing all of the organization's ills. Production blames maintenance, sales criticizes marketing, the deacon board blames the elder board, some family members criticize others, and so on.

In these negative environments, it often seems like nothing will help to reverse the obvious curse of selfishness. Fortunately, a strategic plan, centered in a common mission, can turn the negative into a positive and heal the divisions. Team building will help immensely, but only after everyone understands the organization's purpose and direction.

I once had the opportunity to help a pastor analyze the lack of unity among the staff members of his church. As a result of interviews, I learned that the combatants all truly wanted the church to grow and seemed to have a great deal in common. So what was the problem? We eventually discovered that the source of their troubles was a lack of agreement on the mission. Some believed that the church should be run according to a long list of rules and regulations. To them, any violation of even the slightest rule meant expulsion from membership. Other leaders believed that while some rules were appropriate, there should be ample room for mercy, grace, and tolerance for those yet weak in their faith. Once this significant difference of judgment versus grace was discovered and explained, the leaders were able to work together to forge a new, common understanding of the church's mission. After extensive strategic planning sessions, the majority of the group arrived at a new position that fell somewhere between the original two. Predictably, some of the leaders were unable to accept this revised statement of mission, so they resigned. While this was unfortunate, it was far better than the alternative of extended infighting and confusion and, ultimately, a split congregation.

The Mission Statement

A mission statement needs to have sufficient wording to explain the essence of why the organization exists and what it hopes to achieve or become. All mission statements should contain directional components that clarify *what* the organization does and, essentially, why it exists. This may include information about product specialties, markets, and quality standards. Some mission statements also contain cultural components that address the human side of the organizational equation by defining standards for both internal and external relationships. Here is the mission statement that guides the actions of the employees here at Molitor International: *We at Molitor International <u>demonstrate</u> and teach foundational principles of leadership, interpersonal relationships, and problem solving in order to unleash the dynamic potential in communities, organizations, and individuals.*

Because our work focuses heavily on the development of productive interpersonal relationships, we include both the directional (what we do) and the cultural (how we do it) components in our statement of mission. The directional components clarify whom we work with—communities of all sizes, organizations of all types, and individuals—and that we teach foundational principles of leadership, interpersonal relationships, and problem solving. The cultural aspect of the statement is captured in one word: *demonstrate*. In our mission statement, the word *demonstrate* is underlined for one simple reason: it reminds all of us that if we are not ready to demonstrate any of the foundational principles that we teach, such as caring, integrity, and respect for others, then we are not ready to teach them to others.

Our mission statement accomplishes two things. First, it tells our customers what they can expect from anyone representing

Molitor International. Second, it is a constant reminder of how easy it would be to stray from our course, so consequently we constantly evaluate our own effectiveness, integrity, quality, and commitment. Our statement of mission provides a clear path for us all to follow.

Mission Possible!

New business start-ups usually take the time necessary to clarify and write down their mission statements. However, this process often seems unnecessary to those in charge of existing organizations. The reason? Because they are already doing *something* that occupies their time. Obviously, existing restaurants are busy preparing and serving food to paying customers, hospitals are taking care of the sick, churches are engaged in various ministries, and businesses are making products and/or providing services. Since they are already up and running, does it make sense to take time away from daily operations to clarify the mission and then write down the obvious? While it may not seem like it, the answer is simple. Yes, it makes great sense to take the time necessary to insure that everyone involved shares a common view of the present and future. Remember, what is obvious to some members of the organization is anything but obvious to others. Profits, performance, and commitment can be increased when all personnel are clear on the proper direction and priorities.

> WHAT IS OBVIOUS TO SOME MEMBERS OF THE ORGANIZATION IS COMPLETELY HIDDEN TO OTHERS.

Who Sets the Mission?

The leaders of an organization establish the mission. This is *not* the job for employees or volunteers on a foundational level. This is a common mistake made by well-meaning leaders hoping to generate a sense of ownership among employees. I have worked with numerous organizations that had to demolish mission statements that had been put together by multilevel committees or representatives from various divisions. The intent of the leaders was noble, but the application just does not work. It is analogous to a parent asking teenagers to set the course for the family's success. The teenagers may be competent, willing, and insightful, but that is no substitute for decades of experience and a much more complete understanding of the complexities of raising a family.

Employees should be invited to participate in the organizational process *after* those in leadership have established the vision, mission, and values. There is still ample time for employees at all levels to participate in discussions, problem solving, and decision making on issues that affect their roles, responsibilities, and jobs. The bottom line here is this: the leaders of a nation, community, company, ministry, or family must establish the purpose and direction for that organization. At the appropriate time they will then get input from all other levels and will empower the people below them in the organization to carry out their respective parts of the mission.

Communication Is Key

Once a mission statement is written, it must then be properly communicated to everyone within the organization. During the communication process, the mission statement must be interpreted and personalized so that everyone's performance can be linked and aligned. However, the written statement is the means to the end, not the end itself. That is, it is not sufficient just to write these things on a sheet of paper. Production employees in many manufacturing businesses don't have a clue why top management ever bothered to write down the company's mission statement, because it was never explained to them. But management's credibility and the company's viability skyrocket once the mission statement becomes the guiding light for *all* employee activities. The value of having a clear mission may be experienced on a more personal level as well.

Mission on a Personal Level

I am convinced that the human soul cries out for purpose and remains restless until our lives have real meaning. Since we are multidimensional beings, we function best with a clear vision for all aspects of our lives, including our work, family, health, key relationships, finances, and more. Without solid purpose and direction, we are often like children lost in a crowd, unsure of our next move.

In recent years an amazing phenomenon bears strong testimony to this fact. Rick Warren's best-selling book, *The Purpose-Driven Life*, has swept across America and other parts of the world, motivating hundreds of thousands of people of all ages to spend time determining their essential purpose, direction, goals, priorities, and talents. It provides a clear call to be deliberate about life and to understand two very important facts: first, we are all created for a purpose; and, second, we will be much more fulfilled when we discover and pursue that purpose. It is important to note that the book has not only been read by a narrow group of religious fanatics or midlife malcontents. Its broad appeal has reached to men and women throughout society, regardless of race, age, or nationality. Translated, this means that we are all looking for purpose and direction for our lives. We clearly want and need a mission for our lives. Insightful organizational leaders can utilize this fact for the benefit of everyone involved. This knowledge can transform individual companies and entire communities, as we will explore in the next chapter.

CHAPTER 16

CASE STUDY

Community Development

1000 Leaders
Community Training Initiative

C ommunities today desperately need to release the power of agreement within them. Too many municipalities, counties, and even entire nations waste inordinate amounts of time with infighting, blame placing, and political maneuvering, rather than uniting for the common good. Even in areas that seem hopelessly lost, however, there is still hope that things can turn around. A prime example of this is the community of Saginaw, Michigan.

Saginaw sits in the middle of a county that is rich in farmland, industry, and agriculture. Saginaw County's 200,000 citizens are a wonderfully diverse group of people. At first glance it would seem that all of the pieces are in place for success; yet Saginaw has historically been a divided community, functioning well below its potential. In fact, this county has been known for its disagreement much more than for its agreement. This divided image is heightened by the river that runs directly through the center of the city, splitting it into east and west sides. There are also racial, political, labor/management, and urban/rural conflicts that contribute to the perception of division within the area. Lose/lose/lose.

Various leaders throughout the years have attempted to bring a greater degree of unity and common purpose to Saginaw County. Their efforts have been appreciated by some, scorned by others, and often simply ignored by those who saw them as members of the "other side" rather than as neutral agents of change. The lack of progress created a long-term decline in hope, a rise in crime, and ever-increasing division among the various groups within the country. Things looked quite bleak until a few leaders from the area, in 1999, decided to try something new.

The Plan

All positive change efforts begin with a vision of what the involved leaders want their organization to become or achieve. In this case, Saginaw County was the "organization," and the process for positive change began with the establishment of the vision. As a first step, key members of the Saginaw County Chamber of Commerce introduced a plan called the "Saginaw County Vision 2020 Community Betterment Project." The chamber served as the organizing body or catalyst for a larger initiative that would eventually encompass the entire county.

The next step was to appoint a committee called the Founding Vision Partners to serve as the board of directors over the initiative. This group's research confirmed that Saginaw County lacked common purpose and specific strategies needed for success in the new globally competitive society. Armed with this understanding, the Founding Vision Partners developed a clear vision statement, as well as goals, expectations, and actions that could be pursued and monitored. The goals for the project are listed below:

Goals of Vision 2020

1. Establish a common vision and direction for Saginaw County.

2. Involve citizens of all walks of life throughout Saginaw County to establish common priorities for the county.

3. Develop priority strategic actions, which will address the following areas of interest:

   ❑ Education
   ❑ Life quality, including elderly, health, children, art, culture, recreation
   ❑ Industrial and economic job growth
   ❑ Countywide infrastructure
   ❑ Government
   ❑ Private sector and community leadership

4. Unite citizens throughout the region to openly discuss problems as opportunities for change.

5. Create a structure to ensure that plans developed are implemented.

6. Establish a series of public benchmarks with specific, measurable results that are annually published for public review.

7. Develop an intense communication campaign throughout the county that will allow for total citizen participation.

To help with the process, county leaders secured the services of Henry Luke from Luke Planning Inc. Mr. Luke served as the process consultant for Saginaw as he had done with over fifty other communities throughout the world. Together they communicated the vision to the citizens of Saginaw County as a way of involving them in the process. This was achieved through a series of town hall meetings.

From these meetings came the directional and cultural components necessary to begin to move 200,000 people in a positive direction. The core values agreed upon by community members were recorded in the following manner:

Statement of Core Values

Saginaw County citizens wish to become a united community of excellence. We will develop and use these core values as guideposts to pursue the interdependent vision and strategies. Core values are the character traits that will guide our daily decisions. They are:

- ❑ Positive Attitude
- ❑ Faith in God
- ❑ Integrity
- ❑ Commitment
- ❑ Diversity
- ❑ Entrepreneurism
- ❑ Accountability
- ❑ Creativity

Another important feature of the community's plan involved benchmarks, ways that the project leaders would measure success. Here are the benchmarks for Saginaw County's Vision 2020 Plan:

- ❑ Net new job creation
- ❑ Income growth
- ❑ Quality of life
- ❑ Racial harmony
- ❑ Education

Each year the above benchmarks have been measured and analyzed to determine progress.

What Was Missing?

As good as the plan to rally the citizens of Saginaw County around a common vision and set of values was, there still seemed to be something missing. There was still a tremendous amount of resistance to change on the part of many people, and large segments of the population failed to get involved. Meetings were often attended by the same group of community leaders who had always been in power. This meant that little diversity was evident. In addition, the statement of values proved easier to create than to demonstrate, leaving many of the traditional dividing walls still standing. Something was needed to transform the vision and values into reality.

The 1000 Leaders Training Initiative

In 2002, I met with the president of the Saginaw Chamber of Commerce to discuss the progress of the Vision 2020 initiative. We determined that there was a need for a leadership/relationship development process that would bring together all of the diverse groups in Saginaw. After some discussions, we set an imposing goal of training one thousand community leaders to participate in an advanced leadership-training program. For this reason, the program became known in the community simply as 1000 Leaders.

Input from local banker Gene Pickelman, Chamber representative Liana Bichand, and many others brought the initiative from the vision stage into reality, and soon we hosted our initial training session. A very interesting group from all corners of Saginaw County attended the inaugural three-day seminar. By design, the participants reflected a tremendous amount of diversity, consisting of men and women of five different races, Republicans and Democrats, representatives from labor and management, farmers and executives, as well as pastors and priests.

My staff and I led this group through three days of challenging activities that forced interaction among the leaders of formerly opposing groups. After some initial discomfort, the attendees discovered what we had believed all along: they had more in common than in conflict. During those three days, we watched a marvelous transformation take place. What began as a disjointed group of individuals, motivated primarily by self-interest, soon became a unified team, willing to sacrifice for their community. Over the following months, hundreds of leaders, including the mayor, key business leaders, city council members, township supervisors, heads of banks, religious leaders, and many others, attended the training sessions. Each departed with a new and increased respect for others, a sense of connectedness with people of other races, and a renewed commitment to help their community prosper.

> DURING THOSE THREE DAYS, WE OBSERVED A MARVELOUS TRANSFORMATION THAT WAS TAKING PLACE.

At the end of each seminar, we surprised our attendees with a non-typical challenge. Rather than giving out certificates for attending the workshop, as so often happens, we told participants that they needed to do something tangible before "graduating." We challenged them to select one project for community improvement and to implement that project during the following months. They were then invited to come back to present their project results to a future 1000 Leaders class. When these veteran leaders returned, they would give reports on the success of their projects to motivate and inspire the new class members.

The Results

The results were outstanding! Many leaders chose to work together on projects to improve a wide range of conditions within the county. Here are just a few of the hundreds of projects undertaken:

❑ Develop a Saginaw County Youth Leadership and Diversity program

❑ Develop a countywide arts and cultural celebration to be adopted by the public school system

- ❑ Organize a mentoring program for young girls to teach self-esteem, social skills, and proper etiquette
- ❑ Create an Alzheimer's disease support group
- ❑ Develop a summer recreation program for at-risk children
- ❑ Work with the Bridge Center for Racial Harmony to increase its effectiveness and reach

The list of influential projects goes on. Some are very simple and others are complex. Here are a few of my favorites:

- ❑ Guerilla Gardening – One-person city beautification project where the leader locates vacant lots in the city and plants wild flowers to brighten up the neighborhood.
- ❑ Cross-the-Street Day – One woman organized an annual event where neighbors literally walk across their streets to interact with others, especially those whom they had not yet met. She got local newspapers and radio and television stations to publicize this event.
- ❑ SAGE – Saginaw Area Gardening Exchange, in which east side and west side residents gather to plant vegetables on vacant city land and then donate their produce to the poor.
- ❑ Hearts with Hammers – Project that teaches building skills and home maintenance to young people.
- ❑ Scouting for Seniors – Program to connect young people with lonely senior citizens.

It was very clear that the leaders put a great deal of thought into their projects and understood the complex interrelationships within the community. For example, more than a hundred people got involved in a program called Reading Buddies. In this wonderful program, business leaders donated an hour each week in which they drove to local schools and simply read to and with third grade students. They placed special emphasis on schools and students that had the poorest performance in reading.

Could such an initiative really have a positive effect on a community? Without question! Here is why. National research shows that 85 percent of people in jail *cannot read.* Local research confirmed that Saginaw had several schools where a high percentage of children in the fourth grade struggled with reading skills. All it took was someone to see the connection between literacy and success and the Reading Buddy program was born. Teaching young people in Saginaw to read today will reduce the number of them who will end up in jail in the future. That is vision.

Not surprisingly, other organizations and communities noticed the impact that the 1000 Leaders program was having and got involved. For example, the Dow Corning Foundation donated $100,000 to help offset some of the costs of running the program. Other foundations also donated money to the cause, and the program continues to change lives, revitalizing the community from the inside out.

One of the graduates serves as executive assistant for the mayor of Saginaw and on a task force with the governor of Michigan. She says that as she interacts with people in the community she can tell which ones have been through the program just by the way that they work with others. "There is a freedom of mind and soul that comes from the program," she says. "Gone are the racial hang-ups that used to stop so much progress in our community. Through the training, we learned to make a decision and then never look back. When we did the exercise on *Greatest Leader* and I talked about my own family, I felt a huge burden lift off . . . and I have never been the same!"

> AFTER THE GREATEST
> LEADER EXERCISE,
> I HAVE NEVER BEEN
> THE SAME!

At a recent 1000 Leaders meeting one of the participants stood and asked those in attendance to invite the next generation's leaders to attend the program. She explained that she was in her early fifties and someday would retire from her position of leadership in the community. This insightful woman was already making plans so that the leadership base in the community would remain strong for generations.

The secret to the success of the 1000 Leaders program is really no secret at all. A few committed leaders in Saginaw County rallied around a positive vision, got others involved, learned the skills needed to succeed, and released the awesome power found only in agreement. Talk about a win/win/win!

CHAPTER 17

Core Values and Corporate Character

T he existence or absence of core values sets the foundation for human interaction in every organization worldwide. The absence of clear core values will always lead to trouble. . . .

Just a Flesh Wound

"I've got it!" yelled the agitated employee seated at the end of the conference table. "I'll hide in the parking lot after work; and when the boss comes out to his car, I'll shoot him in the arm. You know—just a flesh wound. Then maybe he'll listen when we try to talk to him!"

No, this is not a scene in an old gangster movie. It was a proposal made by a frustrated employee during a brainstorming session some years ago. This creative gentleman and his coworkers were discussing a problem with the "boss" when the bizarre suggestion surfaced. At the time, I was helping (at least I thought I was helping!) the group design a strategy for improved labor-management relationships. It soon became obvious that the relationship problem between the supervisor and his subordinates had been ignored for years and was about to reach a very tragic end.

The scariest part of the whole situation was that the rest of the group was ready to approve the plan. Tough bunch! After a few seconds I recovered from the shock of the suggestion and redirected the discussion toward the importance of balancing a plan of action with core values. The employee obviously had a plan, or mission (shoot the supervisor), but he lacked the core values (such as respecting and caring for others) needed to prevent a tragedy. If carried out, this plan certainly would have had a lose/lose/lose ending for employee, supervisor, and the entire company. The concept of core values saved the supervisor's skin—and possibly his life, if the employee's aim was as bad as his suggestion.

What Are Core Values?

Core values explain an organization's collective culture and what is deemed as acceptable conduct toward others. They essentially set the standard by which all members of the organization agree to live and work. In the simplest form, core values are the "rights" and "wrongs" as perceived by the individual members of an organization. Statesman Thomas Jefferson is quoted as saying, "In matters of principle, stand like a rock." Once core values have been set, they must never be compromised.

In previous chapters we examined the various components that provide direction for all organizational activities. These include vision, mission, goals, projects, and tasks. Remember, these directional components describe and clarify *what* an organization does. This is a good beginning; for peak performance, however, an organization must also clarify *how* it intends for the human side of the equation to function. In other words, leaders first determine what the organization is to achieve or become (vision/mission) and then they select the principles of behavior and standards (core values) to determine how their people are to treat others, both inside and outside of the organization.

It is important to understand that an organization's culture is established by the attitudes, behaviors, and communications of the people involved. Moreover, what people do and say is directly founded upon their interpretation and adherence to their personal and corporate core values.

Common Core Values

Some common core values embraced within organizations today are honesty, integrity, respecting and caring for others, personal responsibility, and hard work. Unfortunately, not everyone lives by such a code. For example, in some businesses, government agencies, service organizations, and, sadly, families, it is acceptable for people to treat others with disrespect, do shoddy work, and/or put forth less than their best efforts. This typically happens either because there are no agreed-upon core values or because the core values, though agreed upon, largely have been ignored.

Sadly, many organizations and individuals are disgraced each year after they are caught violating the core values of society or of their specific companies. Newspaper headlines throughout the world repeatedly tell of CEOs, presidents, public officials, religious leaders, and others who compromised their integrity and caused the downfall of those around them. Names of organizations that were once held in high regard quickly become objects of scorn. Enron and Tyco fall into this infamous category, with new ones added on an all-too-regular basis. Clearly each of these companies had respectable visions, missions, and goals, but that wasn't enough to avoid disaster for thousands of people. Their sin wasn't a lack of direction, but rather a lack of adherence to established core values.

Every organization has a culture that is made up of its members' shared set of beliefs and behaviors. The modern concept of culture comes from a centuries-old Latin word, *cultura*, which means tending or tilling. It refers to cultivating soil in prepara-

> FARMERS WILL HAVE A VALUABLE CROP BY DESIGN—OR A WORTHLESS CROP BY DEFAULT.

tion for planting. This provides a great image for us as we think about our own organizations. Gardens and fields that have been carefully tended, prepared, and cultivated stand the best chance of growing healthy crops. In like manner, gardens and fields that are largely ignored also produce crops in abundance. The crops from the untended fields, however, are worthless weeds. This is something that farmers and gardeners for millennia have understood. They will have either a valuable crop by design or a worthless crop by default. This lesson is often lost on today's leaders in business, government, ministry, and in the home. We all will have a crop to harvest. Like the gardeners, we must choose either to create a valuable culture by design or be faced with a tangle of conflicting core values, beliefs, and behaviors.

Core Values Are Not Optional

Amazingly, many leaders attempt to operate their businesses, ministries, governments, or families without ever clarifying what type of culture they desire. After more than a quarter century in the field of human resource development, I conclude that people raise or lower their behavior to the accepted standards of their organization, community, or family. Consequently, whenever any organization evolves without the benefit of guiding values and principles, it quickly disintegrates into factions, divisions, and subcultures. Under these circumstances, each member of the organization establishes personal standards of acceptable behavior toward coworkers, customers, and the work itself.

Many organizations throughout the world operate in a state of barely controlled chaos, as employees, volunteers, and others involved set standards of performance that fit their personal paradigms. The negative impact of these diverse standards is profound. Adversarial labor-management relations, sexual harassment, workplace dishonesty, and low customer satisfaction often find their roots in the soil of unclear culture and conflicting core values.

Core Values Are Not Rules and Regulations

The ancient philosopher Plato once said, "Good people do not need laws to tell them to act responsibly, while bad people will find a way around the laws." While he was speaking about society in general, his comment has application for organizations as well. Here is why.

Core values are different than an organization's list of rules or employment policies. Most companies have employee handbooks that outline a wide variety of regulations—dos and don'ts with which every person is to comply. The problem with most handbooks is that, in their attempt to clarify how every situation is to be handled, they become incredibly detailed and cumbersome. This creates a situation in which most employees don't even bother to try to learn all of the policies because there are so many. Those employees who do learn all of them often do so in an attempt to discover loopholes and ways to "beat the system." To make matters worse, excessive rules and regulations are paralyzing to supervisors who quickly learn that they risk the wrath of the rulebook if they make logical work-related decisions about employee conduct when the violation is not clearly spelled out in the book.

Excessively detailed rulebooks also tend to eliminate synergistic discussions among employees and managers alike, thereby squelching the power of agreement. Clearly there is a better way. The problems and challenges that face leaders today require much more than a simple interpretation of "the rules" by some corporate referee. To remain competitive we must solve problems in the framework of an organization's mission and values rather than upon rules that were written in the past by people who failed to see the value of cooperation.

Core Values at Work

As stated earlier, vision and mission deal primarily with what an organization does, not how its members intend to treat others. Therefore, to understand an organization more completely, we must also know its core values if we are to understand the people who work there. The core values may be recorded in a list of individual statements, phrases, or words, such as *honesty, integrity*, and so on. Alternatively, they may be placed in an all-encompassing sentence or short paragraph. For example, Molitor International uses the following statement to highlight our company's core values: *We strive to be known by our customers, suppliers, coworkers, and others in the world community as people of integrity, honesty, caring, respect, faith, and professionalism.* As this statement shows, core values establish an organization's general attitude and approach to business ethics, morality, and interpersonal relations.

Core Values = Collective Corporate Character

Core values reveal the heart and character of an organization as quickly as they reveal the heart and character of a person. Consider this: Adolf Hitler's stated mission for his country sounded good. It included national pride, high levels of employment, and prosperity. At first glance it would be difficult for anyone to find fault with what he proposed. When Hitler's core values are seen along with his mission, however, the entire picture becomes clear, and we see *how* he wanted to accomplish his twisted dream. History reveals that his core values included hatred, prejudice, lust for power, violence, and, ultimately, genocide.

We must remember that core values and mission are inseparable. The mission is the desired end and the core values are an essential means to that end. This has tremendous implications for all sorts of organizations.

Core Values, Morality, and Ethics

Core values are closely tied to an organization's approach to morality and ethics, which, in today's pluralistic world, have become controversial subjects. While neither ethics nor morality can be regulated within a work environment, *standards* of moral behavior certainly can be. In other words, ethics and morality are internal issues that come from what is in each person's heart—only God can change that. However, ethical and moral behavior can be *influenced* within an organization when there are clear definitions of what is acceptable and unacceptable and when people receive appropriate rewards or consequences for their actions.

Some people may struggle with the concept of core values in today's "anything goes" world. They may perceive core values to be too negative, too controlling, and too restrictive. Nevertheless, without values, rules, laws, and boundaries, freedom eventually disintegrates into anarchy. In this state, any and all attitudes, statements, and behaviors become acceptable in the name of diversity and tolerance.

> FREEDOM WITHOUT CORE VALUES, RULES, LAWS, AND BOUNDARIES EVENTUALLY DISINTEGRATES INTO ANARCHY.

Is this an exaggeration of the potential problem with unbridled diversity without the balance of core values? Hardly. In recent history, groups have exercised their diverse religious "freedom" by committing mass suicide, leaving a multitude of grieving family members behind. In addition, consider an example from the new frontier of the twenty-first century: cyberspace. Since its creation, the Internet has grown into a powerful system for communication, information, and worldwide interaction. The teachings, products, services, and personal messages of a growing number of people are suddenly available to the entire world. Innovative global businesses form, long-distance commerce is conducted, new friendships are created, and children learn about the mysteries of science on the World Wide Web. These are all wonderful things, and few would disagree that the Internet is a wonderful tool. However, while the Internet gets an incredibly high grade in its *mission* of worldwide information exchange, it fails miserably in the area of *core values*. Let me explain.

As we entered the new millennium, there were few established standards for what could and could not be transmitted over the Internet. The result? Predictably, people with core values that differ from the norm began to push the decency envelope. Some tried to use computer networks to steal trade secrets and money from other companies. Some used the Web as a conduit to spread hatred against other nations or to preach violence against certain religious groups. Still others used it as an outlet for a wide range of hard-core pornographic materials that were instantly accessible to people of all ages, including children. The degeneration continued as some twisted pedophiles used the Internet to contact young, innocent victims. Naturally, many solid citizens became alarmed and spoke against unrestricted use of such a powerful system. Just as naturally, other people, who opposed any restrictions on what they perceived to be their rights and freedoms, rose up to defend any and all uses of the Internet.

To summarize the point here, the Internet itself is neither good nor bad; it is just a tool or vehicle for information transfer. Governments, communication experts, international lawyers, people of faith, and others eventually will agree on a set of standards to protect network users and still allow individual freedom. When they are finished, the result, although it may called something entirely different, will be a list of core values. The application for organizations is simple and clear. Not everything is good. Not all behaviors are consistent with an organization's core values. Only by clarifying them can an organization hope to maintain proper standards of behavior for its members.

Who Establishes the Core Values?

In order to succeed, the leaders of every organization must develop the list of core values. It is important to understand that this is not a joint project in which every employee, parishioner, or family member gets a vote, nor is it a situation where a simple majority decides what the core values should be. To be genuine, the organization's culture must first and foremost reflect the core values of its leaders. There are many valid opportunities for follower involvement within an organization, as we will explore in later chapters.

Communicating the Core Values

For many years, I have held strategic planning sessions with leaders to help them clarify their core values and then develop strategies for communicating them to the rest of the organization. This second step, communication to others, is essential for establishing or reestablishing an organization's culture.

I had the pleasure of working on this process with a team of executives from a large health care organization recently. Our plan was to design and facilitate a comprehensive cultural orientation process for the organization's four thousand-plus employees. After weeks of planning we created a series of four-hour sessions that included speeches from company officers, fact-filled handouts and brochures, motivating videotape presentations, and a time for questions and answers. The session design even included hundreds of door prizes such as shirts, hats, and gift certificates for attendees.

To accommodate the massive number of employees and allow them to attend during work hours, we had to create a schedule that extended over several weeks. The program content was designed with one primary goal in mind: to provide each employee with a complete understanding of the organization's cultural and directional components. Therefore, in each session we covered the organization's vision, mission, and core values—and specifically how each employee could help to promote these foundational elements on the job. Organizational leaders publicly pledged that they would operate according to the set of foundational core values as they pursued organizational excellence. At the end of each session we presented a long-term developmental plan that included team building, leadership development, mentoring, and other initiatives designed to help leaders and followers alike operate according to the new expectations.

The financial investment was significant, with direct costs exceeding fifty thousand dollars. The organization paid all the expenses, which included the cost of the meeting hall, food and refreshments for the employees, handout materials, and door prizes. It also paid employees for time spent attending the orientation meetings, which cost approximately two hundred thousand dollars. When the final meeting ended, those involved were exhausted by the sheer magnitude of the task.

We naturally asked ourselves the question that every leader should ask after making such an investment: Was the initiative successful? The answer to this question is a conditional *yes*. Yes, the meetings were well designed and facilitated. Yes, the speakers were convincing. Yes, the employees loved the door prizes and were excited about the plan for training and development. Finally, yes, everyone who attended left with a clear understanding of behavioral expectations, and therefore understood the desired corporate culture.

However, the long-term answer can be given only when there is adequate follow-up, support, and accountability for the desired behaviors. If a few rogue managers are allowed to abuse employees in the future, it will not take long for the culture to disintegrate. If a few lazy employees are allowed to shirk critical duties related to patient care, the culture will quickly devolve into less than what was desired. Yet even with this degree of uncertainty, I am convinced that it was well worth the effort. Had we not informed the workforce of the directional and cultural expectations, I can guarantee that the organization would never reach its potential.

Personal Application

An old cliché says, "Everyone has a price." This means that no one is capable of standing firm in the face of temptation. In other words, regardless of how committed individuals are to their core values, they will violate them for enough money, power, or other incentives. I strongly reject that notion and have good reason to do so. In reality, millions of people choose to live by their core values each day despite temptation and opportunity to do otherwise.

We are shocked by the indiscretions of leaders in government, business, church, or family situations for one simple reason: It is not the norm. Not everyone is involved in some sort of scheme, deception, or unethical pursuit. The majority of people, fortunately, live according to a set of standards that guides them through the pitfalls that regularly appear on the road of life. Organizations and individuals that successfully navigate through these traps not only establish core values but also translate those broad values into specific attitudes, behaviors, and communications, called operating principles, as we will explore in the following chapter.

CHAPTER 18

Operating Principles:
Core Values in Action

*H*onesty is a concept that makes it onto most organizations' lists of core values. Honesty provides a wonderful foundation upon which to build a complete list of core values. Without some further explanation, however, this marvelous word could actually cause some trouble. Here is why.

Core values tend to be comprised of single-word concepts that are open to interpretation. Words such as *honesty* often mean different things to different people. As amazing as it sounds, some people will actually take that word to mean that they should tell people anything and everything that they choose, as long as they are being *honest* when they say it. In both the worlds of business and ministry, I have encountered people who felt that they were doing others a favor by telling them that they did not like their ideas, their neckties, and even their race—all in the name of honesty. Were these people being honest with their opinions? Definitely. Were they also being wise, caring, and respectful? Definitely not.

This is why each core value must be expanded upon so that its full meaning can be understood. Here is how this works.

Translating Core Values into Operating Principles

The core value of honesty should be expanded into several sentences that explain what it means for the employees or members of that particular organization. Operating principles typically will be written as "We will" or "We will not" statements. It would look something like this:

Core Value: Honesty

Operating Principles:

> We will not withhold important information from each other.
>
> We will not lie to each other.
>
> We will share our opposing views with each other in respectful ways.

This same procedure is followed for each core value until all have been expanded into operating principles. The sum of these provides clear expectations of how members of an organization are to behave. The combined values and operating principles could also be called a code of conduct.

At Molitor International the core value of honesty becomes a viable operating principle when our associates tell clients the truth about problems in their organizations instead of lying to perhaps gain a lucrative contract. The core value of caring likewise becomes an operating principle as we show respect and concern for each person with whom we work, regardless of his or her position. As a final example, people who work in our corporate offices understand that the core value of respect must be translated into operating principles that apply to

> WRITTEN OPERATING PRINCIPLES TAKE ALL OF THE GUESSWORK OUT OF CORE VALUES.

our support staff as well as people outside of our organization. This means that secretaries are included in decisions that affect their jobs, are spoken to politely, and are never to be subjected to sexual harassment.

This simple procedure of expanding our values into a set of positive principles for behavior has, in effect, created our company's culture. Written operating principles take all ambiguity out of an organization's core values.

Avoid Assumptions

Leaders should never assume that others within the organization automatically understand their values or operating principles. Therefore, it is wise to clarify and present them in writing to employees and anyone else affected by them. Remember, operating principles describe the way in which the core values are to be demonstrated on a daily basis. While they may seem restrictive at first, operating principles have exactly the opposite effect. Without clear operating principles, meetings disintegrate into endurance sessions or grudge matches. Each member of the organization develops his or her own set of principles in order to justify his or her actions. Controlled chaos reigns in this setting until someone steps forward to create a new set of acceptable norms. No organization ever suffered from core values and operating principles that were too clear, but many have died from lack of clarity.

Once clarified, operating principles become powerful tools with which to build a productive organizational culture. One of my favorite clients, a manufacturer in West Virginia, created the following set of core values and operating principles that are widely supported by employees. Their approach was to write operating principle statements that were somewhat broad and then clarify them through extensive discussions with their employees. Here is what they created.

We believe that every employee should:

1. Conduct ourselves in a positive manner.

2. Foster cooperation rather than confrontation.

3. Communicate in a positive and helpful manner—avoid propagating rumors and other forms of negative communication.

4. Promote doing the right thing instead of focusing on one's need to be right.

5. Recognize and appreciate others.

The people who created this list are some of the most strong-willed and independent people I have ever met. They are also some of the most insightful. Both management and union employees recognized that clear core values and operating principles were a way to focus their energies on satisfying their customers rather than fighting against each other. The value of their company has skyrocketed in recent years. I am not surprised.

Without a Code of Conduct, the Mission Is Vulnerable

Once acted upon by its members, core values and operating principles create an organization's culture just as surely as laws and shared beliefs do for a larger society. Conversely, failure to have a shared code of conduct produces disastrous results in organizations and institutions, large or small. For example, over the past few decades I have witnessed the sad decline in the effectiveness of public schools in the United States. To be sure, the vision and mission of the American public school system is stellar. The system was created to teach the next generation how to succeed in life. No one could argue against that. A solid vision and mission without corresponding values is always vulnerable, however, so it is no accident that the school system is struggling.

Not only have our schools experienced a decline in achievement test scores during the past few decades, but also a corresponding decline in the behavior of many students. Some fascinating research shows that in the early 1960s two of the biggest problems with students were tardiness and chewing gum in class. By the turn of the century, things had changed dramatically. It was discovered that two of the most significant problems in school were aggravated assault and the use of illegal drugs. While some external factors such as the breakdown of the nuclear family contributed to this degeneration, I am convinced that one of the greatest contributors to the problem was the removal of the Ten Commandments and other religious references from display and discussion in "public" classrooms. My position here is not based on fundamentalist religious ideologies but rather on my study of shared core values and operating principles. Here is my rationale.

For many generations, every child in the public school system in the United States was exposed to the Judeo-Christian concepts of the Ten Commandments and the Golden Rule of "Do unto others as you would have them do unto you." Chances are very good that many of those children had at least some reinforcement of these teachings in their homes. In addition, before the 1960s children learned that they would experience significant consequences—positive or negative—based upon how well they followed the rules (code of conduct, core values, operating principles) established by the school and other parts of society. The children learned that if they

> AFTER THE 1960'S,
> THE GOLDEN RULE
> HAD LOST ITS GLITTER
> . . . AND STUDENTS
> SUFFERED FOR IT . . .

violated school policy they would receive corporal punishment, such as a swat on the backside with a paddle, be forced to remain after school, and/or be expelled—depending on the severity of the infraction. Again, the focus on accountability and self-control was much more strongly supported in the home in those days. Through constant reinforcement of the code of conduct, students learned that compliance had great rewards and that outward rebellion came with a high cost.

In the final analysis, the existence of clear guidelines accompanied by indisputable rewards for good behavior and certain punishment for noncompliance showed students the beauty of absolute right and wrong. If they proved themselves to be diligent and respectful students in school, it was likely they would obtain good jobs after graduation. This then meant that they would have the means to generate wealth, security for their families, and a great deal of personal freedom.

As motivating as this was, there was one additional concept embraced by students in pre-1960s American schools. That is, people were ultimately accountable for all of their actions to God, a power higher than themselves. Translated, this meant that little Johnny or Mary could anticipate that their deeds, good or bad, would generate a consequence in this life *and* in the life to come.

Exposure to a clear code of conduct for behavior, and to the divinely inspired core values found in the Ten Commandments and Golden Rule, created a set of shared values and beliefs adhered to by a majority of Americans for generations. At the micro level, this code of conduct provided a foundation for student diligence, a basic standard for conduct and morality in schools, respect for authority, and an accepted system of reward and punishment. At the macro level, these shared beliefs helped the American society galvanize around a solid moral code. Again, much has changed since then.

From a values perspective, our schools began to undergo significant changes during the 1960s. Various individuals and groups began a concerted effort to make two fundamental changes in the public school system. First, a new permissive attitude was adopted wherein students who knowingly broke the rules were not punished as before. Second, an assault was launched on anything that had religious connotations. Unfortunately—or fortunately, depending on your position—these people were successful not only at "protecting" students from undue religious pressure but also at removing references to God, the Bible, and the Ten Commandments from school facilities. During this same time school prayer was banned, leaving no doubt in the minds of students that God and a code of absolute rights and wrongs were out and that a new set of valueless values was in. This new code was based on the belief that each man, woman, boy, and girl was capable of developing his or her own standard of conduct.

Some effort was made at the turn of the century to return some of the earlier foundations to our schools, but it was and is a case of too little, too late for the countless thousands of people who, having survived their school years, brought the confused creed of relativism into their places of work. The result? They often have difficulty working together, taking direction from others, and following the rules. Some of these people eventually make their way to the top of companies, and the sad results are predictable. The incidences of worldwide corporate scandal, sexual misconduct, fraud, insider trading, lying, cheating, and embezzlement are at all-time highs, bringing customer and investor confidence to all-time lows. This lack of clear values also contributes to the highest divorce rate in history, as husbands and wives create their own rules for relationship rather than following the historical norm.

To sum up, the vision and mission of the educational system remained relatively constant. What changed dramatically were the values and operating principles that were taught and modeled within the context of school.

Operating Principles, Rewards, and Recognition

As we have seen, core values and operating principles form a code of conduct for all members of the organization to live by. It would be wonderful if simply knowing the expectations would cause everyone to live up to them. However, it does not. Unfortunately, a minority of employees, volunteers, and others often refuse to follow rules and guidelines without some external reward, recognition, and/or discipline. For this reason, leaders need to use their established code of conduct for more than just decoration on office walls. This is accomplished by including operating principles in the organization's performance review process and also in its discipline policies. Doing so establishes two very clear paths upon which employees can choose to walk. Those who perform according to the operating principles are rewarded with merit pay, promotions, and other perks. In contrast, employees who choose to violate the operating principles receive proper attention, counseling, training, and, if all else fails, discipline and/or dismissal.

Another way to help all employees internalize the code of conduct is to make it a prime topic of discussion at every meeting, presentation, and written communication from top executives, management, or administration. Once the behavioral expectations are clear, then employees can choose either to abide by them or to move on. The power of core values and operating principles cannot be overstated. Without a shared code of conduct, everyone chooses his or her own way to act, operate, and behave. This chaotic approach will never bring a group together. Instead, it insures that unresolved conflicts in values will occur and relationships will fracture.

The Foundations Are Laid

Now the organization has its foundations in place. It has a clear vision, and its leaders have created a written statement of mission from which all other activities flow. In addition, the organization's members have diligently developed a clear code of conduct consisting of core values and operating principles. In essence, all members of the organization now know where they are going and how they are expected to treat people along the journey. Our next case study shows how the leaders of a failing educational institution overcame tremendous challenges through the establishment of a new vision and a new code of conduct.

CHAPTER 19

CASE STUDY

Education

Southeastern University

Southeastern University began as a tiny Bible school in Alabama. Birthed in 1935, during the Great Depression, it struggled simply to survive. In those days its student body consisted of a small handful of students that milked cows and did other odd jobs to pay for their tuition. Donations for the school came more often in bushels of turnips than in thousands of dollars. As time passed, the school followed an erratic pattern of slow growth and decline as it wrestled to find its identity and purpose.

In 1952 the school was moved from Alabama to Lakeland, Florida. The change in location did little to change its fortunes, however. Its painful pattern continued for many years until the college reached a defining moment in 1999. Enrollment was down at that time, and for various reasons, the morale, hope, and financial resources at the school were also at record-low levels. Aging buildings in need of desperate repair mirrored the internal problems that threatened to bring the school to an end. At that point school officials faced the very real possibility that they needed to close their doors. Fortunately, members of the board refused to give up hope and saw all of the challenges as one huge shining opportunity. Sound familiar?

The Plan for Success

As their initial step forward, the board contacted Dr. Mark Rutland and invited him to serve as president of the college. Despite the fact that he was successful, comfortable, and happy with his life at the time, Dr. Rutland accepted the task. His challenges to bring a spirit of excellence to the school began immediately and continued for many years.

Dr. Rutland's early days on the job proved to be extremely stressful, as the new president was forced to layoff thirteen employees, many of whom had been there for years. The first external hurdle that he and his team faced was an accreditation process that, had they failed, would have put the school out of business. President Rutland's basic approach to this and every subsequent challenge was to drive people to succeed and then celebrate their successes. This strategy proved effective and the college passed the accreditation process, which gave the school additional time to recover, revive, and retool. Many still believed, however, that it was a matter of too little, too late. Fortunately, through a combination of hard work and inspiring vision, Dr. Rutland and his team brought the college to new levels of success. Here is how they did it.

New Vision, Mission, and Values

Not surprisingly, the new levels of success grew from a systematic approach to change management, beginning with a new vision, mission, values, and achievable goals. The vision for the college was, is, and will continue to be simple: that is, to thoroughly prepare students for success in whatever sphere of life they choose to enter.

Early on, the leadership team established and embraced a

philosophy of consensus building wherein respect for others and open communication were key. As part of this new approach to operations, Southeastern's leaders were instructed and inspired to think systemically instead of narrowly. This approach linked together, rather than divided, all elements of the college. Using this new paradigm, mistakes were viewed as pilot programs yielding valuable lessons for the next attempt. This encouraged innovation, drive, and initiative on the part of all the leaders.

Along with the new vision and leadership philosophy came a clear set of values that were used to benchmark and judge all decisions from that point on. Southeastern began to operate using the following philosophical statement as its guide: *Without vision, you go nowhere. Without values, you go to the wrong place.*

The View from the Top

Dr. Rutland says that his greatest challenge was keeping a unified, transcendent vision in front of all staff. In his view this was and is the preeminent way to keep everyone working together. He further says that his most important function is to constantly remind all members of the staff of their unique roles and vital connection to one another.

To support the new vision and values, Southeastern implemented a new philosophy of leadership as well, one in which employees at all levels are included in making decisions that affect their jobs. Within this supportive environment, each employee is viewed as an expert to be listened to and respected. Leaders at Southeastern believe that their primary responsibilities are to give staff confidence and support rather than harsh directives and unneeded discipline.

This nontraditional approach carries over into the college's interaction with students as well. In fact, the college now takes a unique approach to marketing and attracting new students. It simply asks potential students to answer *yes* or *no* to these five basic questions to determine if there is a good fit between the student and Southeastern:

1. Will a college degree be helpful or necessary in my chosen career?

2. Have I enjoyed and profited by educational experiences in the past?

3. Is it a goal of mine to be an "educated" person in the broadest sense of that rather than to be "trained" for a skill?

4. Do I enjoy being in a community of enriching faith?

5. Do I want to be mentored and challenged at an intimate university?

This approach to student recruitment works well. In fact, the average student enrolling at Southeastern now enters with an astounding 3.5 grade point average!

In a recent letter to prospective students, Dr. Rutland explains Southeastern's culture in just a few easy-to-comprehend lines: "Southeastern is not a huge research university, but a caring community where we are attempting to integrate faith and higher learning. We believe too much of modern education is a slice-and-dice experience that makes students in one major resent taking courses in others. At Southeastern, we are asking hard questions about God and culture."

The Impact of Positive Change

Southeastern has seen some incredible changes during the past seventy years. It grew from a small school, to a struggling college, and then, miraculously, to a fully accredited liberal arts university in 2005. From such humble beginnings, the university has graduated over thirty thousand students, has thirty-five undergraduate majors, including premed and theater, and now offers graduate degrees as well.

While the university has retained its original spiritual roots, it has allowed them to spread in a wide variety of ways. Southeastern now features an extensive roster of community activities, such as Student Body Leadership Council; resident life; national honor societies and academic clubs; outdoor clubs and special interest associations; groups for married students and off-campus students; newspaper and yearbook; cheerleading; and offshoots of their state-of-the-art communication facilities, SC Radio and TV Channel 11. As a member of the NCAA, Division II, Southeastern fields teams in men's and women's basketball, men's baseball, women's volleyball, men's and women's soccer, women's tennis, and men's golf.

Changing Young People – Changing the World

From its early days as a tiny school in Alabama, the university has grown into an institution that is changing the world. Its graduates are encouraged to impact culture through a lifestyle of excellence and integrity. In 2004 the student body represented forty states and ten foreign countries, so the potential of this institution influencing the world is easy to grasp. Not only do its students touch lives after graduation, but during their college careers as well: by getting involved with projects to the elderly, troubled teens, unwed mothers, the homeless, battered women, and persons with disabilities, as well as hospital visitation, crisis intervention, and music and drama ministry.

In a time when so many young people are focused solely on themselves, Southeastern has found a way to get them looking at the world around them—seeing the needs and then implementing strategies to meet those needs. This institution is a prime example of what can be accomplished when inspired leaders agree upon innovative ways to combine faith, vision, values, and the power of agreement to overcome the challenges of our world.

PART FOUR

Developing the Human Side of the Organizational Equation

CHAPTER 20

Education and Training: Keys to Success

"**Y**ou can't teach an old dog new tricks!" smirked the young know-it-all from the back of the conference hall. "Our company should just get rid of all the older employees. Lots of them don't even have college degrees and seem pretty stupid! They don't want to learn anyway."

I had just finished presenting a plan for cultural change to his company's management team and had asked for comments. Big mistake! This junior executive was armed with a new MBA degree, expensive leather suspenders, and lots of theory—but lacked any real-world experience. That is a very dangerous combination. He was challenging my recommendation that all employees be involved in training to help eliminate the adversarial relationships between labor and management. I confess that I have a difficult time remaining civil when confronted with this sort of prejudice, so my response to him was pointed.

"First," I said, "I don't know who would appreciate a new trick more than an old dog. Second, each of the older employees represents an investment of approximately one million dollars to your company. It would be very foolish to throw that away. Third, education does not equal intelligence. The employees whom you are so anxious to discard have had the intelligence to run this place for years without too much involvement from people like yourself. If you think about it, they literally are in charge of the entire operation on second and third shift, when most managers have gone home for the night."

> I DON'T WHO KNOW WOULD APPRECIATE A NEW TRICK MORE THAN AN OLD DOG.

By this time, the young executive's smirk had morphed into a frown, but at least he was listening. "Finally," I said, trying to regain my composure, "the whole issue of *respect* comes into play here. You should remember that these employees are the ones whose hard work and sacrifice over the years have made it possible for you to even have a job. They deserve a chance to learn and enhance their skills the same as you do."

With that, he sat down, I calmed down, and we went on with the meeting. Afterward it occurred to me that this zealous young man was a lot like the preacher who was so heavenly minded that he was no earthly good. His ideas made no sense in the real world. Senior management fortunately accepted the recommendation and requested the training for all employees. Not surprisingly, the results were tremendous. The older employees proved the young critic wrong as they excelled in the training and played an active role in that organization's change effort.

The Wisest Investment

In recent years, organizations in the United States alone have invested some sixty-five billion dollars per year in workplace education and training. Not long ago the Gallup Organization released a survey that showed some interesting facts about this subject. It indicated that 84 percent of employees who received at least six days of training within the previous year said they were satisfied with their jobs, compared to only 70 percent of those who received no job training. In addition, 80 percent of the people surveyed said that the availability of company-sponsored training programs was a factor in deciding whether to accept a new job with another organization or to remain in their current positions.

In today's world, education and training are no longer options; they are now necessities. Just as no organization can afford to allow its technology or equipment to become obsolete, neither can it allow its human resources to become outdated. We must upgrade each employee's skills, knowledge, awareness of new technology, and aptitude for human relations. In the race for corporate survival, we must equip our people with the skills and confidence to solve problems—problems that don't yet even exist.

Preventive Maintenance . . . for Relationships

In recent decades an amazing shift has taken place concerning preventive maintenance. Gone is the old practice of running equipment until it completely breaks down. This destructive practice has been replaced by revolutionary new preventive maintenance policies that initially seemed counterintuitive. The pioneers of this practice faced stiff opposition from doubters. Shut down equipment that is running properly? Can that possibly make sense?

Eventually these policies were instituted in countless organizations that had machines, equipment, and/or technologies that were capable of unpredictable breakdown. Some wise person discovered that it made more sense to invest time performing minor repairs, upgrading technology, and maintaining equipment at regular intervals—even when things were running properly—than to mindlessly wait for random breakdowns to occur.

Clearly we need a similar mindset change concerning our human resources. Perhaps we should paint employees a neutral color and attach power cords to them as a reminder that relationships can break down at the worst possible time, leaving an organization to flounder. I recall a pilot strike that occurred in the late

1990s that cost one airline more than two hundred million dollars. I guarantee that some preventive maintenance performed on the relationships between management and the pilots *before* the strike would have prevented a sad waste of money, time, and energy.

To achieve this new mindset we first must realize that money spent on employee education represents a wise investment rather than just another cost. In fact, it is the wisest investment that organizational leaders can make. People are the only resources that have such limitless capacities to think, reason, innovate, problem-solve, and plan.

Corporate University

I encourage our clients to think of their organizations as "corporate universities" in which each member of the organization can function as both teacher and student. In this setting every person watches for opportunities to learn and grow, as well as to teach new skills to others. With the corporate university concept, employees and volunteers are not satisfied with the status quo but constantly look for ways to expand their knowledge about a wide variety of topics, including products, services, customers, suppliers, markets, and especially their competitors. They replace the old adage, "If it isn't broken, don't try to fix it," with one of their own: "If it isn't broken, let's see how we can make it better before our competitors do!"

Remember, organizations are often staffed by members of several different generations. Some of them may have entered the workplace during their late teen years and others when they were middle-aged. Regardless of when they arrived, many will remain until retirement in their sixties. This provides compelling reasons for virtually every member of an organiza-

> IF IT ISN'T BROKEN, LET'S SEE HOW WE CAN MAKE IT BETTER . . . BEFORE OUR COMPETITORS DO!

tion to participate in workplace education programs. No one wants merely to exist in a job that has no sense of newness. Employees today are no longer willing to endure years of monotonous motion with no promise of excitement or innovation in their jobs. They want to participate in their jobs, have positive interactions with coworkers, and enjoy company-sponsored continuing education as part of their employment. The list of courses that will benefit employees and employers alike is endless. It includes training in technical areas, customer service, communication, leadership, computer literacy, supervisory skills, problem solving, and a wide variety of human relations training.

The Goal of Education and Training

The goal of workplace education and training is very basic. It is to equip people with the relevant information, knowledge, and skills necessary to be productively involved in the accomplishment of the mission—in ways that are consistent with the values. Therefore, training must be designed to build support for the change process and enhance employee competence as it progresses.

As I reflect on the organizational assessments that we have completed during the past quarter century, there are three areas on the human or cultural side of the equation that consistently require education and training. They are leadership; team building, or interpersonal relations; and problem solving. These areas represent some of the most foundational skills and principles needed for change, growth, and excellence among employees. Leadership training ensures that executives, middle-level managers, and supervisors are prepared to initiate the change process. The team-building/interpersonal relations training equips people at all levels with the skills necessary to work effectively with others. Finally, problem-solving training empowers people with skills to address problems, make decisions, and develop effective action plans as they press toward the mission. Following chapters will provide more details on each of these training topics.

Good Employees: Hire Them or Train Them?

Interestingly, a primary complaint of executives and managers around the turn of the century was that it was difficult to find workers for their operations. Even with several billion human beings on earth, their problem was not one of scarce resources but rather the lack of *qualified* or *properly trained* individuals. Since then some companies have formed partnerships with local educational institutions to better prepare employees before they enter the workforce. Others have hired the best people available and then put them through rigorous education, training, and development programs of their own design. Both approaches have worked extremely well. Despite this fact, there are still many leaders today who gladly spend millions of dollars on new technology or equipment but balk at spending a comparatively small amount on employee training and development. This makes little sense.

Management by Gut Feel?

Several years ago I spoke with a business owner who failed to see the value of employee training. Over lunch one day he boasted about the huge sum of money that he had recently spent on a new computer system that would "revolutionize" his midsize manufacturing operation. His grand vision was one in which every aspect of his company would be computerized, including ordering, manufacturing, accounting, inventory control, and so on. His vision for change was a good one, since up to that point record keeping was inconsistent at best. He explained that historically inventory counts were often kept on small scraps of paper and manufacturing runs were often based on the supervisor's "gut feel" rather than actual data. It sure seemed like the computerization was a great idea, except for one small problem. This manager decided that his employees only needed a single day of training on the new system, because the thorough training program recommended by the experts was too expensive. One day! It takes longer than that to learn how to play a child's video game! Lose/lose/lose.

The result of his folly was predictable. His employees gave it their best effort; however, after several months of frustration with technology that seemed to work against them, they began to bypass the computer system to get some work done. Once again inventory counts were done on scraps of paper and supervisors used gut feelings as their guides for production runs. For peak performance, we clearly need to upgrade both our technology and our interpersonal capabilities as well.

Reaching Heads *and* Hearts

In today's world there is a need for education and training to go beyond basic skill development or reinforcement. Effective training not only must impart new skills into the learners' minds but also touch their hearts. For example, one common problem in the corporate world today relates to communication—at least many problems are categorized that way. Countless training sessions are designed each year to teach people the basic skills and techniques of communicating with others. Unfortunately, many of these sessions are a complete waste of time and money. Here is why.

Attendees file into classrooms, listen to instructors, and practice how to organize their thoughts and then speak clearly to their coworkers. At the end of the training session they march back to their workstations and discover that their communications are no more effective than they were before the session. Why? Because often the real problem with corporate com-

> IT'S NOT THAT PEOPLE DON'T KNOW HOW TO COMMUNICATE; THEY JUST CHOOSE NOT TO COMMUNICATE.

munications is not that people don't know *how* to communicate, but rather that they choose *not* to communicate. The solution here deals more with influencing people's wills than upgrading their skills. In addition, too many people simply don't understand how to develop and maintain the healthy relationships required for effective communication in the work environment. They often are insensitive about the impact of their words on others, and this is rarely covered adequately in a training seminar focused on "communication."

The One-Day Wonders

I recall a warehouse manager who was having a terrible time with employee morale and productivity. Although I took several days to interview his entire workforce, the cause of his problems was easy to see by the end of the first morning. I learned that sixty days prior to the assessment, the manager had attended what I call a "one-day wonder" training session where he learned "all that he needed to learn about management"—or so said the flyer received in the mail—in less than eight hours. The manager left the training session with just enough understanding of several concepts to be dangerous to his employees' morale, his organization's success, and his own career. It seems that he had learned a new term called *value added* at the seminar. From that day on he felt compelled to include the term whenever he addressed his employees. Unfortunately, his message came across in the worst possible way. One day he literally told members of his staff who worked in the warehouse that their function was not considered "value added." Naturally the employees were hurt, angry, and demotivated by his insensitive and inaccurate comments. This gentleman's problem was not one of basic communication. Believe me, his employees understood exactly what he was saying. Instead, he showed a lack of understanding of human relations when he failed to anticipate *how* his message would affect his employees.

To be clear, I favor teaching communication skills. My company has done so for years. However, it is infinitely more important to teach people how communication influences their *relationships* with others than it is to teach new techniques of speaking and listening. For some, this message is a welcome confirmation of what they have always believed. For others, it is a shock to their insensitive systems. Effective training must prick the conscience of those who chose not to treat others with respect, kindness, and common courtesy if we truly are to improve communications within any work environment.

The Order of Education and Training

For maximum effectiveness, training must be conducted in the proper sequence. That is, it should begin at the upper levels of the organization and progress downward. It is important for leaders to participate in all culture-related training programs that are commissioned following an organizational assessment. This empowers the leaders with firsthand information about the training and shows their commitment to the change process. Failure to follow this sequence can be disastrous.

I recall a large church whose leaders invited us to assist them with a staff development project. The church's effectiveness was hindered by a serious lack of unity among staff members. After some initial discussions we designed a series of weekend workshops to address the relational breakdown that had occurred, to create open lines of communication, and, in theory, to give them a new start. Our team walked into the church building on the initial morning of the training with high hopes and great expectations. It took less than five minutes for those hopes to be shattered, which was the exact amount of time it took the senior pastor to address the group on the relevance of the training—and then tell them that he had "important matters" to attend to and walk out the door. As he left the room, so did any hope of unifying his staff. Their attitudes changed from mildly interested to surly, and the workshop became a test of endurance. Key leaders must always be active in the training process!

It is important to understand the fundamental goal of any training initiative. This is especially true when it comes to "leadership" training in an organization. The goal is to link and align the mission, values, and foundational practices of all leaders by providing them with a united paradigm concerning leadership. This does not by any means suggest that everyone must speak and act exactly alike; there is plenty of room for individual personalities. However, there must be agreement among all leaders on the foundations of leadership and on how leaders will interact with others on a daily basis. It is the lack of alignment and agreement among leaders that causes division and weak spots to occur within organizations. This is why leadership training and development must include all leaders, at every level, starting at the top and moving downward.

> LEADERSHIP TRAINING MUST INCLUDE ALL LEADERS, STARTING AT THE TOP AND MOVING DOWNWARD.

Middle-level managers and supervisors often benefit greatly from training in leadership and interpersonal relations. Why? Although top leaders design and communicate the mission and core values, the middle managers and supervisors actually bring them to pass by their daily actions. It is much easier to create a mission than it is to live it and achieve it.

Once those in positions of authority have received training, it is time to include the remainder of the organization. My experience proves that foundational-level employees excel in training sessions that are based upon an organizational assessment. Countless times I have witnessed the incredible transformation that occurs when employees are given the opportunity to learn new skills.

They develop a sense of pride in having learned the information and eagerly apply it at work and in their personal lives.

Three Keys to Effective Training

Clearly education and training are integral parts of any change process, since there is a need to upgrade both technical and human relations skills continually. Unfortunately, not all training procedures are successful. I have found that the most effective training programs share three common traits. First, the training is a part of a long-term approach to change, not a quick fix that is soon forgotten. I do not believe in a training blitz in which everyone in an organization is rushed through a few seminars and sent back into an unchanged work environment. It is much better to have individuals attend no more than three days of relevant training at a time, then practice what was learned for several weeks before attending another session.

The second trait of successful developmental programs is that the training is practical rather than theoretical. All practical information obviously has its origin in theory. However, trainees should not have to sit through hours of lecture on the theory of relationships or leadership, or anything else for that matter. Instead, they should be given a brief introduction to a topic and then move quickly into learning practical lessons that address actual organizational issues. The training subject matter should always be aligned with needs identified during the original organizational assessment or subsequent surveys. This way the training comes as a solution to agreed-upon problems rather than as a random program with no basis for implementation.

The third and final characteristic shared by effective programs is that the training is always highly participative as opposed to lecture-based. Adults interested in positive change tend to be people of action who readily respond to an opportunity to interact with their peers. Education and training built upon short teachings, simulations, small-group discussions, and team projects capture the attention of participants and help to insure that maximum learning takes place.

The Future of Training and Development

In the future, the need for high-quality training and development initiatives will increase. The reasons for this include stress, downsizing, pressure to perform, worldwide competition, global teams trying to work together, stress, new technology, computer innovations—and did I mention stress?

In tomorrow's world, technology, equipment, regulations, roles, and relationships will continue to do two things: change and increase in complexity. This reality requires that people be properly trained in a myriad of areas or they will fail, thereby putting the entire organization in jeopardy. While training and development require an investment of time, money, and other resources, there is simply no other way to insure maximum competitiveness. Properly designed and implemented training programs result in a "win" for everyone involved—company, leaders, employees, and customers.

Remember, while we humans show signs of wear and tear as we age, we will never become obsolete. Our next case study describes an innovative approach to the training and development of future leaders in the health care industry.

CHAPTER 21

CASE STUDY

Health Care Merger

Covenant HealthCare System

M y analysis of Covenant HealthCare System's effectiveness began at 3:00 A.M. on March 17, 1997. That was the moment I received a phone call informing me that my father had suffered a life-threatening heart attack and was being rushed to the hospital. As if in a bad dream, I hastily dressed and drove forty miles to join other tearful family members in the hospital's waiting room.

The events that followed, which were nothing short of amazing, taught me much about the importance of health care professionals and the profound impact they have on our lives. What I did not know at the time was that two years later my company would be hired by Covenant to assist them in developing their new corporate culture. What began as a tragedy ultimately led to one of the most exciting health care projects with which I have ever been involved.

At the time of my father's heart attack the name of the hospital was St. Luke's Health Care Association. A new entity, Covenant Hospital, was about to be created by the merger of St. Luke's and its former competitor, Saginaw General Hospital. Each had an impressive history of providing quality care to its customers before they officially merged on July 1, 1998 to form one of the largest health care organizations in Michigan. Combined, their workforce rose to nearly four thousand people in a wide variety of positions.

Life and Death

Tests showed that my father had several blockages in the main arteries of his heart, so he was scheduled for emergency quadruple bypass surgery. After the lengthy operation was performed, my dad was taken to a recovery room to sleep off the anesthetic. My family breathed a collective sigh of relief as a smiling hospital chaplain entered the waiting room and informed us of Dad's positive progress. His good report released an abundance of pent-up fears and tears from worried relatives. It was such a relief to think that he had made it through his surgery and life would soon be back to normal. Or so it seemed. What we did not know was that the ordeal was far from over.

Twenty minutes later the chaplain reappeared at the waiting room door. This time his face was ashen and he explained in hushed tones that something was terribly wrong. My father had been rushed back into surgery. There the doctor had to reopen his chest cavity to stop some internal bleeding and to address new complications. The hospital staff prepared us for the worst. My mother, other family members, and I prayerfully waited as tense minutes turned into exhausting hours. Finally, at 8:30 P.M., the surgeon was once again finished and my father was moved back into a recovery area. I later learned that the doctor had canceled two other scheduled operations in order to stay with my father during this critical time.

What followed were some of the most stressful days that the Molitor family has ever endured as Dad hung on the edge of eternity. He was placed on extensive life-support systems since he was unable to breathe for himself. Like angels in blue scrub uniforms, the nurses in the cardiac care intensive care unit watched over him twenty-four hours a day. Although my father was unconscious, they encouraged us to visit him. During these brief periods I observed that the nurses were both kind and competent.

The following weeks brought me into contact with hospital administrators, doctors, nurses, cafeteria staff, and volunteers. With very few exceptions, these people showed tremendous competence and sincere concern for customer satisfaction. I am thrilled to write that twenty-one days after his heart attack my father was able to return home, with a new appreciation for both health care professionals and life itself.

> THESE PEOPLE
> TRULY CARED!

During one of my follow-up visits to the hospital, I arranged to meet with the chief executive officer, Spencer Maidlow, and other executives to learn how they had achieved such a fine operation (no pun intended). I also wanted to thank them personally for doing such a fine job of caring for my father. As we spoke, I was not surprised to learn that their success was no accident but was the result of careful planning and hard work. I also learned that the only thing constant about the health care business is change!

Soon after our meeting, Mr. Maidlow invited me to assist Covenant with their merger plans by creating and implementing a long-term developmental process for all four thousand employees. I gladly accepted.

The Merger Process Begins

Once the merger project was underway, I learned about each organization's culture and approach to training and development. This background information was extremely helpful as we designed the plan to unify the workforce at all levels. I was amazed at the amount of work that the people at Covenant had to do to make the merger a success. Although their two cultures were similar, some major problems still needed to be addressed—not the least of which was the fact that the employees, who had been competitors for many years, were now expected to work together as a team. In the health care business, this was literally a matter of life and death. In addition, because each hospital had been a full-service provider, there were duplicate departments, units, and staff positions.

Regardless of the challenges, we knew that there was only one logical place to begin the project. The new group of leaders had to determine Covenant's vision, mission, core values, and operating principles. Once these were in place, all other decisions became much easier.

The following are Covenant's actual statements of vision, mission, and values. Note that some of the statements combine elements of mission, values, and operating principles.

Our Vision Statement

A promise of caring—A commitment to service

Our Mission Statement

We bring together the people, the caring cultures, and the values of our founding hospitals into a renewed commitment to building an accessible, comprehensive healthcare network serving Michigan. In fulfilling this commitment, we are guided by the following principles:

- WE commit to providing exceptional care through competence, compassion, and spiritual and ethical values.

- WE maintain financial strength while encouraging risk taking and exploration: creating solutions to anticipate and meet the changing needs of our environment.

- WE believe alignment and integration of our corporate entities, teams, physicians, and providers of care are required for the success of our network.

- WE support an empowered and accountable workforce that embraces change in the pursuit of excellence.

- WE reach out to the communities we serve through the development of healthcare enterprises, wellness programs, and the provision of care to our communities.

- WE support research, education, and technology, and have an evolving role in helping our communities to improve their health.

- WE value a workforce that is diverse and representative of the communities we serve, and we strive to understand and appreciate our diversity.

Our Values Statement—WE CARE

- **W**orking together—We understand that teamwork is the foundation to our success. We diligently work together as a team while balancing work and home life.

- **E**xcellence—We strive through empowerment to do and be the very best in all of our endeavors.

- **C**ustomer service—We recognize that our very existence is to serve. We commit to an unsurpassed level of service to all our customers.

- **A**ccountability—We are responsible to our communities, our organization, and to each other.

- **R**espect—We display a high regard for the personal dignity, diversity, and the uniqueness of those served and those serving. We treat all others as we want to be treated.

- **E**nthusiasm—We project a spirit and attitude that is positive and optimistic. We seek to find good in all people and all situations.

Once these directional and cultural statements were created, it was imperative that they be communicated to all employees to the point of understanding. This was accomplished during a series of cultural awareness sessions. During these four-hour meetings, employees were treated to presentations, videotapes, and printed materials that addressed both the past accomplishments of the two separate hospitals and the plan to forge one united organization for the future.

> THE LEADERS WANTED TO CREATE A TRUE TEAM ATMOSPHERE—WHERE TRUST AND MUTUAL RESPECT WERE MORE THAN WORDS ON PAPER.

Next, they shared the cultural and behavioral expectations for leaders and team members alike. This list of attitudes and actions left little doubt that Covenant leaders wanted to create a team atmosphere in which trust and mutual respect were more than just words on paper. Most employees left the sessions with a mixture of optimism and anxiety. This was to be expected due to the fact that, because of the merger, many of their responsibilities, working conditions, compensation plans, and reporting relationships would change in the subsequent months.

The Role of Training and Development in the Merger

Immediately after the orientation sessions we customized a long-term plan for education and training for all levels of the organization. This was to ensure that the values and expectations would become reality in the daily work lives of employees. The creation of the plan was complicated because it needed to include thousands of people, from three shifts, who worked at many different locations. Soon, however, we designed the training plan and began to systematically implement it. The plan essentially follows the outline of this book, so I will not rewrite it here.

In general, the developmental plan for Covenant included training in the topics of leadership, teamwork, communication, listening, managing change through proper employee involvement, plus many others. In addition, my staff provided the entire management team with personalized leadership coaching to assist them with their many challenges. As with all organizational change efforts, we observed that some leaders and employees made swift adjustments to the new work environment while others needed more time. This was to be expected. No successful organizational change initiative is easy, but the successful ones all utilize a predictable process. Covenant was no exception.

The Results of the Merger

It has been more than ten years since the merger, and Covenant continues to produce excellent results in bottom line, human relations, and customer relations categories. Since the time that the two hospitals became one, Covenant has participated in a customer satisfaction survey that measures their performance against other hospitals throughout the United States. They have consistently scored in the top 20 percent in all categories and their nursing component is consistently in the top 10 percent of hospitals involved in the survey.

Clearly the merger has produced some innovative methods to improve both performance effectiveness and customer satisfaction. The accomplishments of Covenant employees are impressive and seemingly unending. Because the leaders chose to implement a systematic process of change, this organization has capitalized on the power found in agreement.

CHAPTER 22

Leaders:
Champions of Change

One morning, this sign appeared on the employee bulletin board.

> **ATTENTION**
>
> Starting Monday morning, employees are not allowed to work together when loading trucks.
>
> Signed,
> The Management

At first the employees thought that it might be a prank. Closer inspection, however, confirmed that the sign signaled an official change in policy. Two neophyte managers had placed it there to address what they saw as serious problems within the work environment. Little did they know that the problems were just beginning.

I became aware of the sign, its origin, and the turmoil that it caused during an organizational assessment that I conducted for this building supply company. It turns out that these fledgling "leaders" were sons of the company's owner, who had been placed in charge of the entire operation several weeks earlier. This was clearly a recipe for disaster since they were in their mid-twenties and had no formal preparation for the task. In their new roles, these young men were supposed to supervise a group of intelligent, self-motivated employees, many of whom were more than twice their age.

During the assessment interviews, employees explained that they had initially tolerated their new supervisors because of loyalty to the company owner, who historically had been a good man to work for. Their patience ran out the day the sign appeared, however, and the company was on the verge of a crisis. The rationale for the new policy? It seems that the trouble began when the young supervisors observed two employees laughing as they loaded unwieldy building materials onto a flatbed trailer. Laughing at work: imagine that!

Despite the fact that the work was accomplished well and on time, these immature leaders decided that employees having fun working together simply could not be tolerated! Therefore they instituted the policy that forced each employee to load the trucks alone. Naturally the workers were furious about this decision, and responded with what I call "malicious obedience." In other words, they followed the new guidelines even though they knew it would be bad for the company. Lose/lose/lose.

As weeks passed, the previously profitable company began to falter. The work pace slowed dramatically, causing productivity to fall. Simultaneously, the cost of damaged goods skyrocketed, since much of the material required two men to stabilize it during the loading process. Lost-time injuries began to mount as employees strained backs and tempers trying to muscle unwieldy items onto trucks. And how did the new supervisors respond to the problems? Not very well.

Amazingly, this downturn of events caused the young supervisors to respond in ways that addressed everything but the real problem. They held company-wide meetings to talk to employees about the need for *them* to do "better" work. Next,

> ONE BAD LEADERSHIP DECISION CAUSED ALL OF THE TROUBLE.

workers were forced to watch generic safety videos and listen to lectures on the importance of productivity. At times the frustrated supervisors even scolded employees for not working "smart" enough, and on one occasion the word *lazy* was subtly mentioned. Employee morale plummeted to its lowest level in company history.

I later learned that neither the company owner nor anyone else in senior management was aware of the offending policy until the assessment revealed it. Once it came to his attention, the owner got involved and the situation began to turn around. Eventually the embarrassed young supervisors were forced to change the unproductive course of action, but much was lost in the interim. Productivity, morale, customer satisfaction, safety, management credibility, and workplace unity were compromised during the novices' unrestricted reign of organizational terror. One bad leadership decision caused all of the trouble, or perhaps more accurately, one decision made by unprepared leaders caused all of the trouble.

Who Was to Blame?

To be fair, I don't place the blame for this fiasco solely on the young managers. Following the initial assessment, my time spent coaching them confirmed my suspicions. They had been thrust into their positions with little preparation from their own leaders.

Senior managers gave them a few cryptic sound bytes upon which to base their leadership decisions. Statements such as, "Show 'em who's boss!" and "Give 'em an inch and they'll take a mile!" shaped the thinking of these young men. Because of this the dangerous duo viewed the essence of leadership as maintaining strict control over the workplace. No wonder they interpreted employee laughter as the first stage of an impending rebellion.

Could this negative situation have been avoided? Of course! Imagine the difference if top management had taught these young men some foundations of effective leadership *before* putting them in charge of their company's most valuable resources. Something like this:

> **Senior manager:** "Look at Bill and Jim over on the loading dock. Man, they sure know how to load delivery trucks. They have been doing that successfully for years. Our customers never complain. Those guys are the best! They have a good time at work, too. I love to hear them laugh. You know why? It means they are happy. Isn't that great? As their supervisor, you just be certain that the men have what they need to succeed and everything will work out fine."

These few words and a little ongoing support are all it would have taken for the young men to begin the transformation from immature power mongers to effective leaders.

Leadership Is the Foundation for Success

Organizations succeed or fail primarily upon the effectiveness of their leaders. This does not mean, of course, that other members of the organization are not important. We have already established that fact. It does mean, however, that a group of good employees or volunteers trying to follow a poor leader stands little chance of succeeding in any venue.

Leaders must carry the vision, demonstrate the core values,

and still have time to motivate, listen to, communicate with, and cheer on the rest of the people involved. The higher the position of leadership a person has, therefore, the more crucial it is for him or her to be visibly supportive of the direction and culture of the organization. This is especially true during periods of uncertainty or when a change process is underway. Presidents, plant managers, pastors, and parents are the ones who cause the process to succeed or fail in the initial stages.

This creates an interesting challenge for individuals who achieved positions of power or influence using less than positive methods. While I believe that a majority of those in leadership are solid citizens, I must acknowledge that our world has more than its share of people who lied, cheated, and stole their way into power. For example, some leaders have risen to high positions by deliberately hurting the careers of rivals within the organization. Others learned that the best way to "lead" was to embarrass and belittle others, thereby making themselves look better. Still others found that telling "small" lies to acquire new customer accounts would catapult their performance past that of their peers.

> LEADERS MUST FIND WAYS TO GAIN THEIR FOLLOWERS' TRUST AND COMMITMENT.

One of the most common approaches to advancement embraced by many executives, managers, supervisors, religious leaders, and others is a command-and-control style of leadership in which they are the absolute rulers of their domain. This leadership style may have been appropriate for hardened veterans in combat, but it is hardly suitable in today's ever-changing world. The leader who fails to comprehend that times have changed may find himself at an early retirement party—held in his honor.

The old-fashioned, dictatorial type of leader may succeed temporarily in a relatively stable environment where followers can be closely monitored. These types of power holders are ill-equipped, however, to actually lead when conditions become more challenging and/or when their employees' complete commitment is needed for the organization to prosper. In these settings and circumstances, leaders must find ways to gain their followers' trust and commitment. Failure to do so condemns everyone to struggle for survival in a frustrating, unproductive environment.

It is important to remember that leadership is fundamental to the success of any type of organization. Production is managed; projects are supervised; people are led. There are no magical techniques to motivate those who know their leaders don't care about them. Conversely, there is no end to what followers will attempt for leaders who show that they truly care.

The Heart of the Matter

Clearly leadership is more of an art than a science, and it is infinitely more than simple techniques or strategies to get others to perform—so that the leader looks good. Instead, it is a complex combination of attitudes, behaviors, and values that are consistently applied to the pursuit of a mission. Add to this the sincere desire to serve others and you have the foundations of effective leadership.

While leadership is one of the most challenging and frustrating undertakings on earth, it is also one of the most rewarding. Moreover, I am convinced that anyone can learn to be an effective leader if he or she chooses to do so. Those who answer the call to lead will discover that the gap between frustration and reward is generally quite small; nevertheless, by applying a few foundational principles most leaders can stay closer to the reward side of the equation.

> THE MOST CRUCIAL AREA FOR A LEADER TO FOCUS UPON IS THE ATTITUDE OF HIS OR HER HEART.

With all that is written these days about the subject, it may be difficult for people to decide what their top leadership priorities should be. Goal setting? Communication? Budgeting? Problem solving? Planning and organizing? These are all good and certainly part of a leader's toolbox. None of them comes close to being the most important, however. After teaching this subject for more than a quarter century, I realize that the most crucial area for a leader to focus on is the attitude of his or her heart. Specifically, do they see the position of leadership as an opportunity to be served or to serve others? Do they truly care about those who work "for" them? That is the heart of the matter. This element is missing in far too many discussions about leadership.

Do You Care?

At some point in every leadership seminar that I facilitate I ask the attendees one simple question about themselves as leaders: *Do you truly care about your employees, volunteers, or congregation?* This forces them to consider whether the people they lead are viewed as human beings, filled with dynamic power to change the world around them, or as something less than that—perhaps no more than names or numbers on paper. The room usually gets quiet as the leaders ponder their responses. Fortunately, a large number of them realize that they do care about others within their organizations. A smaller number recognize that they had never thought about it before. Amazingly, and mercifully, an even smaller number admit that they really *do not* care about others and only see people as a means to a better bottom line or to further their own ambitions.

Leadership Development

The practice of leadership is without a doubt different than management, administration, or supervision. While all of these organizational functions are important, only leadership deals with a person's ability to influence, motivate, and guide others in the accomplishment of the mission. Since this is true, it is amazing why so few educational institutions prepare people to actually lead others in the real world. Only recently has there been any significant movement toward the development of leadership skills in the world's colleges, universities, business schools, and seminaries. The result is several generations of people in power with little ability to lead. Often recognized in business and government sectors, this lack of leadership is also common in religious institutions. Too many churches are directed by clergy who are able to prepare and deliver wonderful three-point sermons yet they cannot assign a simple task without browbeating their subordinates.

With all of the options available today for solid education, training, and development in leadership, it is difficult to comprehend why anyone would fail to get the help they need to succeed. Now here is the good news. The skills that leaders need today can be learned by anyone willing to put in the time. I have seen countless executives, managers, supervisors, pastors, and parents over the years change their approaches to leadership and become recognized as outstanding leaders in their fields.

Finding the Perfect Leaders

Organizations that want to employ effective leaders have two options to secure them. First, they can search the world to locate the best leaders alive today. Of course this means that they must somehow locate that tiny percentage of people with natural leadership abilities, charisma, and intuitive insights into all aspects of life, all wrapped in a package of unyielding integrity and unconditional caring. Does this sound like an impossible task? It probably is.

The basic problem with this fantasy is that, here on earth, the "perfect" leader exists only in our dreams. We humans enter this world with a wonderful combination of God-given gifts and talents. However, in just a few short years—certainly by the time we enter the workforce—we also develop a full range of misconceptions, prejudices, weaknesses, and bad habits. If an organization's strategy for obtaining its leaders is limited to hiring only perfect candidates, they will be disappointed. It simply is not going to happen.

The second, and infinitely better, approach is this. Yes, identify the best leaders available by use of proper screening and clear parameters. Then, only select candidates who, through education and previous work experiences, have demonstrated at least some of the desired qualities. Once they are hired, make no assumptions about their understanding of the organization's expectations for leadership performance. Instead, have senior members of the organization sit with each new hire and clearly explain the vision, mission, core values, operating principles, and specific responsibilities for his or her position. Then, improve the new leader's performance over time with training and coaching to enhance his or her skills as needed. Finally, tangibly reward solid performance, swiftly correct poor performance, and if some individuals cannot or will not meet the expectations, release them to find a better fit for their talents.

> THE PERFECT LEADER EXISTS ONLY IN OUR DREAMS.

The foundational point here is this: effective leaders can be developed using a systematic process of training, evaluation, feedback, and coaching.

The Connection between Leadership and Mission/Core Values

The term "leadership" means different things to different people. This is one fundamental reason that leadership practices vary greatly from person to person. For this reason, the first step in the leadership development process is to clarify the organization's expectations for appropriate leadership behavior. Failure to do so would be likened to asking a sharpshooter to hit a bull's-eye without first providing a target. He may use up a lot of ammunition and make a lot of noise, but he will never succeed.

Leadership expectations should always spring forth from an organization's statements of mission, core values, and operating principles. This is why it is vitally important to complete each step of this organizational development process *in sequence*. Each builds on the previous step and is done in preparation for the following step. Consequently, if you skip one step you will have major problems later in the process. For example, some organizations launch leadership-training programs without first establishing a clear mission or set of core values. This always results in a program of general leadership concepts that are taught without any long-term context. Bad idea. Waste of time and money. Conversely, once the mission and values are clear, then clear expectations and a proper leadership-training course can easily be created.

Clear Leadership Expectations

For greatest impact, the leadership expectations should be written either in bullet points or in a series of sentences describing the desired behaviors. One of our recent clients chose to accomplish this by first selecting five broad categories of leadership expectations: strategic thinking, character, interpersonal skills, job performance, and results. Then they wrote a description of each characteristic, explaining how each could be demonstrated within the work environment. Here is how they described the first leadership characteristic, strategic thinking:

> Strategic thinking signifies the ability to be creative in leading a work group toward a target or goal. A strategic leader uses current knowledge and skills, and also is able to think outside of current practices, roles, and conditions to create new solutions.

Similar descriptions were written for the four remaining characteristics. Once the leadership expectations were clarified and recorded, they were shared with all organizational leaders. A training program then was designed and implemented to insure that all leaders possessed the skills needed to demonstrate each quality. This simple yet vital process helped create a positive work environment in which leaders were consistent and competent in their duties.

Evaluation of Current Leadership Effectiveness

Once the mission and core values are clear and the leadership expectations are established, then it is time to evaluate the effectiveness of current leaders. It is only logical at this point to determine if the current leaders are demonstrating the values and meeting the expectations. In most organizations, some leaders are excelling, and others are struggling to meet at least some of the newly identified expectations.

It is important to realize that those failing to demonstrate the expectations may not solely be to blame. Often managers, supervisors, and others in authority perform poorly because they have never been taught a better way to lead. If they were fortunate enough to serve under leaders who taught them to care for and respect their followers, then they are likely to succeed in today's world. If, however, they suffered under a command-and-control or otherwise unprincipled leader, they will need some education, training, and coaching in the foundational principles of effective leadership.

Leadership Coaching and Mentoring

To a casual observer, leadership probably seems a lot like playing golf. What can possibly be so difficult? Just stand there and hit the little white ball with a long stick, right? Not exactly. The game of golf is much more difficult than it appears. Every novice who tries it soon learns the value of instruction from an experienced golfer. Coaching often means the difference between success and failure. A good coach points out the subtleties of the game that separate average golfers from great ones. It is much the same with leadership. We can all use some help perfecting our leadership "swing." Why? Because many leaders are not aware of their mistakes, so they continue to lead improperly. Unfortunately, the longer you practice something incorrectly, the harder it is to change. We must often first *unlearn* our mistakes and eliminate bad habits before we can learn the proper way. This is why many managers, supervisors, administrators, pastors, and others in positions of leadership ask for help in the form of personal coaching.

Through the years, I have witnessed the transformation that takes place when leaders, young or old, receive unbiased coaching and mentoring from someone outside their organization. More senior leaders frequently have no one within the organization to provide honest feedback on their performance. This leaves them alone to try to figure out ways to improve. On the other end of the spectrum are young, relatively new supervisors, managers, pastors, or administrators who are zealous to make a difference. But unless their zeal is tempered by coaching and counseling, these well-meaning people often cause harm to those around them. On the bright side, when young leaders receive proper instruction and ongoing feedback on their performance, then they can spend a lifetime successfully influencing others.

The Result of Increased Leadership Effectiveness

The importance of leaders operating at peak performance cannot be overstated. Remember that leaders must motivate, encourage, correct, and guide every other person in the organization during the change process. Virtually everything that leaders do and say will be analyzed by others to see if it supports the mission, core values, and operating principles. The smallest deviation will be seen as a lack of the leader's commitment to change. If the lack of commitment is perceived to be widespread among leadership, the change process will die a painful death.

As leaders, we should be grateful for the concepts of continuous learning and continuous improvement and for the reality of external competition. Without them we easily could become satisfied with the status quo, set in our ways, and ultimately lose our effectiveness. If we are willing, we can learn to be better leaders every day. Even the "old dogs" can learn new tricks through targeted education, training, and coaching from others. Once learned, these new tricks begin a wonderful chain reaction. The education and training result in increased leadership effectiveness. Increased leadership effectiveness causes an increase in trust, loyalty, and commitment from employees, volunteers, and others. It also produces a willingness in these key members of our organizations to learn about and change their own attitudes, behaviors, and work performance. The result is both satisfying and certain: mission accomplished!

CHAPTER 23

CASE STUDY

Corporate Leadership College

*Corporate College of
Leadership Excellence*

I n 2002 a unique new college opened its doors. It had no ivy-covered buildings, no long enrollment process, no mascot, and no pipe-smoking professors wearing tweed jackets. Instead, the initial course was held in a local hotel conference room and the class size was limited to six students. The "professors" were actually the chief executive officer and the chief operating officer of Covenant HealthCare Systems, one of the largest hospital systems in the Midwestern United States.

Called the Covenant College of Leadership Excellence, this innovative approach to leadership development transfers the wisdom and insights of its top executives to hundreds of other executives, directors, managers, and supervisors within the organization. After taking their company through our Power of Agreement process years earlier, the leaders at Covenant wanted to find a way to keep their competitive edge and motivate their nearly four thousand employees. In response, the Covenant College of Leadership Excellence was born.

The Possible Dream of Excellence

This college concept provides a powerful and progressive tool for keeping the dream of excellence alive. Rather than sending a few leaders off to random seminars each year to learn conflicting approaches to leadership, the college allows each leader to learn directly from a team of in-house experts. This approach insures that the organization's leaders are linked, aligned, and committed to a common vision and values. Molitor International was invited to work with the leaders of Covenant to create the curriculum and the final design for the college. Here's how it works.

The college runs one three-day session each quarter. Students come from many different areas of the health care system. On the first evening, the group spends time getting to know one another at dinner. After dinner, members of our staff lead them through a series of team-building exercises designed to break down barriers and develop openness within the group. The following morning, we lead students thorough a series of exercises to learn advanced techniques of group problem solving, communication, and decision making. Following these team-building activities, Covenant's CEO, Spencer Maidlow, and COO, Edward Bruff, begin a series of short teachings that expose students to various aspects of life at the top of a complex health care organization. These key leaders show wonderful transparency as they speak in detail about the best and worst leadership decisions that they have ever made.

One of the goals of the college is to develop a close bond and open communication between the top executives and other leaders. To facilitate this we have each student share lunch or dinner with either the CEO or COO, in order to have some one-on-one time with him.

Covenant College is designed with a dual purpose. First, it builds productive relationships among all of Covenant's leaders and exponentially accelerates leadership development. Second, it very clearly brings all leaders' ideas to bear on bottom-line improvements in quality, customer service, productivity, waste reduction, and more. To this end we have attendees prepare presentations on innovative projects to increase some aspect of Covenant's performance. On the third day of the college these projects are presented to the group for critique, input, and, ultimately, approval. The project scope is remarkable and the level of innovation is impressive. During recent sessions the students suggested improvements in customer service, pharmacy operations, new methods of patient intake, enhancing staff/physician relations, and many others. I find it amazing that all of these innovative ideas were latent within the leaders themselves, but none would have been discovered or implemented without the forum of Covenant College.

Once the new ideas are presented at the college, the students begin implementation of their projects back at work and then record the results. Ninety days later, these students return to the following session of the college to present their final results to the next group of students and to graduate officially from the program. Graduates receive a diploma, a monogrammed sweater, and a beautiful plaque acknowledging successful participation in the Covenant College of Leadership Excellence.

Following graduation, many of the executives, directors, and managers are invited to return and share their experience and wisdom with their coworkers in the classes that follow. As with all successful projects involving change, the college project began with a vision and some foundational thoughts about what was to be accomplished.

The Results

This project has been extremely successful in both building productive relationships and improving the organization's performance. The leadership has implemented scores of innovations that improved customer service, productivity, quality of care, and more. Covenant's bottom-line indicators have continued to improve since the inception of the college and show no sign of slowing. Here are some of the projects that have been implemented by the students:

- ❑ Proactive preventive maintenance program for all Covenant facilities. This matrix serves to schedule renovation projects based on materials and space usage. This will improve both the physical and perceptual image of the health care system and be useful in long-range budget planning for renovations.

- ❑ Adoption of corporate purchasing card as a means to acquire best prices on goods and services. This would automate many transactions and eliminate the need for purchasing and accounts payable staff involvement, thus leveraging their time for more important tasks.

- ❑ Create screening clinics in the community to identify individuals at risk for cardiovascular disease and provide education that will reduce factors that cause heart disease.

- ❑ Develop a computerized scheduling solution, which would reduce time, minimize scheduling errors, and improve personnel tracking for the Nutrition Services management team.

- ❑ Project Campus Pride – Create volunteer opportunities to assist with grounds keeping and facility cleanliness. This program targets wholesome groups like Boy Scouts, Girl Scouts, and qualified high school students. The project will result in a cleaner hospital environment and a positive work experience for youth.

Edward Bruff, Covenant HealthCare's chief operating officer, sums up the experience this way:

> Covenant College is one of the ways that we're able to develop future leaders at Covenant HealthCare. After each program, I walk away with a higher degree of confidence in Covenant's future because of the leadership talent we have in place. It is obvious by the end of each session that we have alignment around our vision, values, and leadership expectations. Covenant College is improving the quality of life for our patients through the Significant Improvement Projects that each participant is required to complete. Whether it's improving the way medications are administered to neonatal babies or reducing surgical site infections to an all-time low, we're making a difference in the lives of our patients and their families that is very rewarding.

Covenant College is a great example of a win/win/win. The organization wins through increased productivity, quality, and customer service; leaders win by having contented, self-motivated employees; members of the workforce win by having ownership in their jobs; and certainly customers win by receiving excellent health care service.

CHAPTER 24

Building the Team

Team building plays a significant role in the development of any positive corporate culture. As we will explore in this chapter, many people need at least a refresher course in how to work effectively with others. Others need to start over from the very beginning. But here's the good news: once all the members of an organization are skilled in the foundations of teamwork, they can truly release the power of agreement on a daily basis.

Can't We All Just Work Together?

For the past few decades there has been a great deal of talk about team building and related concepts. Along with "team building," terms like "teams," "teamwork," "employee involvement," "empowerment," "natural work groups," and "affinity groups" became part of corporate jargon during the 1970s and continue with us today. With all the buzz about teams, many organizations joined the cause and tried to build teams. Unfortunately, many of them knew just enough about team building to be dangerous to themselves and their employees. Some eliminated their existing organizational structures to form "team environments." Others commissioned groups of people to solve problems and called them "teams." Still others scheduled some basic team-building train-

> OTHERS RETURNED TO
> THEIR ORGANIZATIONS
> LIKE MOTHS SEEKING
> A FLAME.

ing without any real plan for how to make the training part of daily work life.

All of these efforts gave an appearance of progress without making any real improvement in the organization. Of course, with all of the interest (and corresponding money) in this concept, a small army of team-building consultants and trainers sprang up like mushrooms to "help" the process. For a while it seemed that every unemployed manager with minimal experience felt qualified to consult with others about the fine points of team building. Public team-building seminars were offered by the thousands, each event promising to teach attendees everything they need to know about building teams. All of this for ninety-nine dollars or less—with coffee and donuts included. Some attendees learned the basics of team building, ate the donuts, and returned to work a bit wiser. Others returned to their organizations like moths seeking a flame. They immediately tried to force their peers to get with the team-building program, but to no avail. Within weeks their initial zeal was incinerated, since those around them had not the foggiest idea of what all the fuss was about.

Sending a few representatives to a team-building seminar is as illogical as sending just the husband to marriage counseling and expecting him to save a troubled marriage by himself. It just won't work. True team building takes place when *groups* of people learn to work together more effectively, not when a few enlightened people begin talking about it.

> TYPICALLY THERE
> WAS A LOT OF INITIAL
> EXCITEMENT . . . AND
> THEN THE PROGRAMS
> FAILED.

Many companies realized the futility of the piecemeal approach to cultural change and simply plunged into wholesale team-building initiatives without any outside assistance. The results were mixed. Typically there was a lot of initial excitement. Just as typically, the programs failed. The reason for the early excitement is simple: just the thought of teamwork is highly motivating for most people. Deep in our hearts we earnestly desire to cooperate with others and to be part of something larger than ourselves. This produces some initial success—or at least enthusiasm—for nearly all team-building efforts. Without a clear understanding of the entire concept and a long-term, comprehensive plan for implementation, however, these initiatives are bound to fail. Organizations that involve people in cooperative programs without first building supportive relationships offer a cheap imitation of the genuine life-changing concept.

Doing Teambuilding?

My staff and I have worked with many organizations that were experiencing problems with human relations and/or bottom-line performance. When we broach the subject of team building we often hear corporate leaders and union officials alike say, "We have already *done* team building here." But in most of these locations, amazingly, the fact that they have done "team building" has done little to actually create *teamwork*—which was the goal in the first place. We have learned to interpret their comments to mean they did some *training* that they called team building and/or they put a few people into committees that they called "teams." To them, that was *doing* team building. Team building, in reality, involves infinitely more than just a few off-site meetings. Ultimately, teamwork results when a critical mass of employees (at all levels) focus on a common mission and then work together to accomplish that mission using an agreed-upon set of values.

In actuality, team building was, is, and always will be a very complex undertaking. It should not be viewed as an end in and of itself. It should be seen, instead, as the solution for a clearly identified problem within an organization. Team building should be undertaken as a means to empower all members of an organization to do two things: work together to accomplish the organization's mission and understand how to demonstrate its core values during interactions with others. Unless a team-building program is designed and presented in a manner that accomplishes both tasks, it will fail to provide much real benefit to those involved.

Over the years, I have learned that a team-building initiative alone is rarely sufficient to make lasting improvements in any organization. As we have seen in previous chapters, an organization needs a number of elements in place for it to succeed. These include having clear purpose and direction, effective leadership, core values, operating principles, a strategic plan, adequate systems, open communication, and more. No amount of training can compensate for glaring deficiencies in these other areas. When team building is one component of an overall developmental effort, however, it becomes the glue that holds the entire process together. Used in this manner, team building *will* produce incredible results in morale, productivity, and personal performance improvement.

> TEAM BUILDING BECOMES THE GLUE THAT HOLDS THE WHOLE PROCESS TOGETHER.

So What Is a Team?

My working definition of a team is *two or more people who are prepared, equipped, and committed to work together to achieve a common purpose.* This definition makes known that a team may be a family, school system, corporation, or even a nation that seeks to maximize its influence and effectiveness. In addition, a team may be an entire organization or just a part of the organization. For example, the members of a local church, including the leaders, can be considered a team. However, subgroups within the same church can also be considered teams. There may be teams of ushers, teachers, preschool workers, maintenance personnel, deacons, and elders who help achieve the overall mission as they complete their own group's goals.

Food for Thought

Here is a simple truth: in the vast majority of cases, people working in effective teams accomplish more than an equal number of people working individually. True teamwork produces benefits in both productivity and personal satisfaction.

Years ago I heard one man's account of heaven and hell. Interestingly, he described hell as a banquet hall filled with millions of people. They were seated across from one another at tables covered with the most scrumptious food imaginable. Tantalizing sights and tempting aromas filled the hall. There was one problem, however. The handles on the eating utensils were four feet long and could only be grasped at the very end. This made it virtually impossible for people to feed themselves; they couldn't get the food into their mouths. Their frustrations soon grew into anger and rage that lasted throughout all eternity. Lose/lose/lose!

So much for hell. Then the man described heaven. At first glance heaven seemed similar in every respect to the warmer place to the south: it contained the same type of banquet hall, the same wonderful food, and the same long-handled utensils that could be grasped only at the very end. However, the people at the heavenly banquet tables were content. Instead of angry cries, laughter filled the hall. Close inspection showed the reason for their joy. Rather than trying to serve themselves, the people used their utensils to serve someone across the table, who would then return the kindness.

While this story will never win a theological debate, it does make the point about teamwork. We get more accomplished when we work together and when we look for ways to serve those around us. Amen.

Teamwork or Work Teams?

Confusion about the goal of a team-building effort is common. Here is why. The concept of *teamwork* deals with new attitudes and enhanced interpersonal relationships. Conversely, the concept of *work teams* relates more to new structures and reporting relationships. Obviously, there is a huge difference between the two. Companies throughout the world often arrange their employees in a wide variety of new configurations, including modified pyramid structures, multidisciplinary task forces, self-directed work groups, product teams, and cross-functional work teams. People in these new structures may fight like cats and dogs and yet still be called a "team." All too often these new structures yield few positive results. The real value comes when organizational leaders find ways to develop *teamwork* among the members of their organizations. Regardless of the structure or configuration of the employees, once people learn and apply the principles of effective teamwork, then all heaven breaks loose. Then—and only then—are they able to achieve peak performance, as they communicate, listen, respect, trust, resolve conflicts, and solve problems together.

Stand Together . . . or Fall Apart

Teamwork is actually a byproduct of effective interpersonal relationships among human beings. The behaviors and qualities related to teamwork include interdependence, cooperation, caring, communication, listening, and respect for others. Although most of us experience these qualities with friends and family, too often they are absent in our organizational relationships. In part this is because we send confusing messages to our children in their developmental years.

In millions of homes around the world, parents teach their children to cooperate, share, and bond. Selfishness is frowned upon; concern for others is encouraged. This happens for the first five years or so. Then these children enter school, however, and are taught to do their *own* work and are instructed *not to share* information with others. Suddenly competition is not only encouraged but rewarded. The children receive individual grades on report cards, individual honors for achievement, individual scholarships, and, ultimately, individual job offers. So why are we surprised that our organizations are filled with people who aren't sure how to work

> SUDDENLY COMPETITION IS NOT ONLY ENCOURAGED, BUT REWARDED.

together or even if they should work together? This is one reason why having clear core values and operating principles is vital for every organization. These statements clarify expectations about the company's approach to teamwork, thereby releasing, encouraging, and, in some cases, warning employees about the need to work together.

Teamwork Can Be Learned

Through countless training sessions I have found that people must be convinced that it is to their advantage to work together with peers. We should make no mistake that, for many people, cooperation with others is not natural. It is a foreign act that must be taught and reinforced continually after the training has been completed.

Several years ago I designed a business simulation that proves the futility of internal competition and the value of teamwork. We often use this simple simulation as the initial training exercise in our seminars. It works like this: First, we create a mythical corporation, complete with products, schedules, and financial concerns. Then, we divide the participants into different corporate divisions. After that, each division interacts with others in a business scenario that produces either a profit or loss.

The exercise is designed so that individual divisions make money whenever they compete against each other. Whenever one division gains, however, it causes another division to lose a corresponding amount. Invariably the divisions work against each other in the early stages of the exercise, resulting in anger, frustration, and mistrust. Eventually one division risks cooperating with the others, and, *if* the others catch on, they all begin to prosper. Following the exercise we talk about the impact of internal competition on the participants' actual organization. Once they see how "normal" and damaging it is to compete internally, most commit to overcome this tendency and cooperate for the benefit of all.

The Foundations of Teamwork

Team-building training and development should focus on the primary elements of teamwork. Over the past quarter century, I have discovered that the most effective teams share the following foundations.

Clear Purpose and Direction

Each team member must understand the team's purpose and direction in order to maximize his or her contribution to the mission. This includes an understanding of the organization's mission, primary goals, core values, operating principles, and, finally, the role that each team member is to play in the organization's strategic plan. On a micro level, each person must understand why his or her specific team has been formed and what they are expected to achieve.

Effective Leadership

Team leaders generally determine the pace and performance of a team. Each team has different leadership needs, so I use the term *effective leadership* to allow for a variety of approaches. Some teams need a great deal of instruction, guidance, and oversight. Others need a lot of freedom to accomplish their tasks. It is up to the team's leaders to determine what is needed to optimize its performance. Effective leadership is crucial because team members can never compensate for or outperform incompetent leaders for an extended period.

Productive Interpersonal Relations

When people work cooperatively together, a dynamic power—the power of agreement—is unleashed. The greater the cooperation, the faster the organization can change. Conversely, in organizations where there is little teamwork and poor interpersonal relations, change is painfully slow. Real teamwork is easier to describe than to achieve, since people often tend to be independent and self-centered and need time to develop trust in others. It takes a lot of hard work to develop unity between just two individuals. Each additional person added to the mix exponentially increases both the problems and potential of the team. Clearly organizations do not automatically unify merely because its members share a common corporate name and work under the same roof.

Communication/Listening Skills

Each member of an effective team is skilled in verbal communication and listening. Some years ago a 150 million-dollar satellite became galactic garbage when it did not properly eject from its booster rocket after launch. According to the manufacturer, it failed to separate properly because the miscommunication between two workers caused the wrong chamber to be wired for separation. Ironically, this flying failure was supposed to be a "communication" satellite. Since words and concepts are subject to interpretation, we cannot eliminate miscommunication entirely. Nevertheless, with proper training, coaching, and feedback on the communication process, we can dramatically improve chances for success.

One very important aspect of the communication process within teams is effective listening. Without it, organizations suffer from an overabundance of information being sent but little actually being received and used to advance the mission.

It is often necessary to remind even the most senior members of an organization of the importance of these basic topics. At first glance, foundational teachings may be considered too elementary for high-level leaders, but our organizational assessments have proven many times that top officials miscommunicate by speaking above their followers' level of comprehension or, worse yet, by speaking down to them. This creates countless interpersonal and performance problems that easily could have been avoided had the proper communication skills been in place. Conversely, employees who understand how to communicate effectively with and listen to their peers, leaders, customers, and suppliers add tremendous value to their respective teams.

Problem-Solving, Decision-Making, and Planning Skills

As individuals, we develop problem-solving, decision-making, and planning skills through training, education, and life experiences. We use these skills each day to avoid life's pitfalls and to achieve personal goals. Since this is the case, it should be easy to solve problems with other people on the job, right? Not exactly. It is a challenge to combine the insights of two or more individuals for numerous reasons. Personal agendas, unchecked egos, poor data-collection methods, and the lack of a systematic approach to problem solving are just a few causes of poor performance. In successful teams, people have learned to use interpersonal skills and group problem-solving techniques to attack organizational problems rather than one another. Throughout the world, an incredible amount of time is wasted in meetings in which participants are unable to solve problems, make decisions, and plan together. Once problem-solving teams are trained, they can quickly resolve complex issues that drain the vitality from their organizations.

Trust-Based Relationships

People today are less trusting than in the past, and for good reason. We have often placed our trust in people who later disappointed, deceived, or demeaned us. In recent years we have seen the downfall of leaders in the political, business, and religious arenas. Millions of people who entered into marriage have found that their "partner for life" was not serious about their wedding vows. These betrayals produce wounds that we wear as we enter into new situations and new relationships. I believe we must teach people, therefore, how to be trustworthy and how to trust others in the workplace. Ultimately, we must learn to forgive and let go of the past as well.

Team members can develop trust as they discuss goals, concerns, and personal values with one another. Granted, it takes time and honest communication to close the book on some of our past hurts and disappointments; but it *can* be done. Trust is born in a team-oriented work environment when we establish an agreed-upon set of core values and operating principles. Trust then matures as team members demonstrate their concern for the well-being of others and work together to accomplish the mission.

Productive Methods of Conflict Resolution

Conflict is normal in any relationship; and if conflict is handled correctly it can be extremely positive. We often choose destructive methods of addressing the conflicts that arise in our organizations, however. While there may be many variations, there are really only five options to choose from to resolve conflict. The first four leave much to be desired. I may ignore conflict, concede to the other person's position without any discussion, force the other person to accept my position, or develop a middle-of-the-road compromise that actually satisfies no one. Poorly resolved conflicts always lead to a lose/lose/lose outcome.

Many have discovered that the best approach to conflict resolution is one of cooperation. This method encourages everyone involved to share their perspectives, facts, issues, and opinions without trying to drag others to their side or position. Handled in this manner, truth—rather than emotion, politics, or intimidation—resolves the conflict. Training is typically required to teach a cooperative approach to conflict resolution. Once trained, a team will see the vast majority of their conflicts resolved to everyone's satisfaction.

Proper Skills, Knowledge, and Abilities

A team's good intentions and positive team spirit can never overcome a lack of skill or knowledge on the part of its members. When my sons, Christopher and Steven, were in junior high school, I had the pleasure of coaching their basketball team. During one tournament, we were scheduled to play against a team that looked like they would be difficult to beat. Our opponents entered the gymnasium wearing designer warm-up suits in matching colors, and their game uniforms were obviously very expensive compared to our team's plain blue shirts. Their coaches, who barked orders to the young men as if they were competing in a world championship, strictly controlled the team's pregame activities. At first glance, things looked bleak for our boys.

When the game started, however, things changed. Despite all of the outward appearances to the contrary, our opponents didn't have the basic skills necessary to compete with our team. They made many fundamental mistakes; and when it came to pure athletic abilities, the boys on our team were far better. We won the game handily.

The application to organizational life is simple: all members of the team must have the skills and abilities necessary to complete their tasks well. This should be a primary concern for all team leaders who want to win their own type of corporate championship.

Sufficient Resources, Information, Supplies, and Equipment

Let's stay with the basketball analogy for a moment. Imagine the results of the contest if I had sent our team onto the court without basketball shoes. What if some of the players were barefooted, and others wore heavy work boots? Rather than cotton shorts and shirts, what if our players wore long pants and overcoats? Let's make it really ridiculous. What if I had them wear woolen mittens while trying to dribble, pass, and shoot the ball. To make matters worse, what if I, as their coach, failed to tell them which plays to run or what positions to play? Under this scenario, who would win the game? Obviously our opponents would. Why? They were well-equipped, had good coaching, and possessed all the information necessary to compete.

All too often, teams in business, government, and other organizational settings lose for similar reasons. Every team member needs the basic equipment, information, and other resources to get the job done properly. Those who have them generally win.

Performance Evaluations, Recognition, and Reward Systems

Here is a foundational truth: teams are formed to *do* something. For example, teams in manufacturing operations produce products. Teams of firefighters put out fires and save lives. Teams in restaurants provide both a product and a service by serving food to their customers. Teams that fail to produce tangible results should be disbanded (or perhaps recommissioned as political committees so that their lack of productivity won't be noticed as much!). The point is this: each team's efforts ultimately result in a product, a service, vital information, or all of these being delivered to some sort of customer.

The quality, timeliness, and value of the products, services, or information provide the basis for the team's performance evaluation and rewards. Team members need leaders to provide clear expectations, feedback, recognition, encouragement, and tangible rewards for their efforts. The best teams receive feedback on their performance regularly. These actions keep the team motivated and operating at peak performance.

PART FIVE

KEEPING THE DREAM ALIVE

CHAPTER 25

Strategies for Long-Term Success

Now is a great time to look back and celebrate how far our organization has come. We have a clear vision and a motivating mission, so our direction is set. We have completed a comprehensive organizational assessment and know our strengths and weaknesses. A strategic plan has been created to maximize our strengths and minimize our shortcomings. Within the strategic plan are new goals, projects, and tasks for each member of our team, so we know where we are going and what we hope to accomplish along the way.

Great progress has been made on the human side of the equation as well. Our leaders have sharpened their skills through training and coaching. Each leader interacts with others in ways that are consistent with our organization's core values and operating principles. Lines of communication are now open from top to bottom and side to side. Caring and respect for others differentiates our organization from our competitors. Team members are empowered and have both the skill and desire to succeed. Problem solving, decision making, and planning are now shared responsibilities, which leads to outstanding customer service and growth.

At this point our organization is moving forward as never before and the future looks bright. We have taken time to celebrate our success and reward those around us for their contributions.

Life is good. So what is next? Is it time to sit back, take it easy, and declare "mission accomplished"? Not exactly. The reason why can be summed up in a single word: change. As we have learned throughout this book, change is constant and we must never allow it to catch us sleeping on the job.

LIFE IS GOOD . . . SO WHAT'S NEXT?

Fundamentals for Continued Success

Here is the great news. The progress made so far can be sustained indefinitely . . . *if* we are watchful and prepared to respond to any situation that could jeopardize our success. Just as there was a systematic process that took us to the top of the mountain, there is also a process that can keep us there.

For continued organizational success, there are two fundamental elements that must be considered and addressed on an ongoing basis. They are critical issues and competitive opportunities.

Critical Issues: Threats to Organizational Success

Critical issues are negative conditions that threaten some aspect of our organizational success. They often develop without warning and may spring up from inside or outside of the organization. Some critical issues are somewhat predictable, such as year-end taxes and seasonal variance in customer buying patterns. Other critical issues, however, arrive on the scene without any warning and require immediate, emergency attention. New government regulations, tougher quality standards, lawsuits, and the emergence of new competition for market share all must be addressed quickly, confidently, and professionally.

Ready for some good news? Handled correctly, critical issues have the potential to become a blessing in disguise. In fact, many increases in productivity, quality, customer service, or some other area often spring forth from what originally seemed like a disaster. In other words, the potential exists to turn the problem into an opportunity for growth.

This is more than just semantics, as one executive found out some years ago. It seems that the company's top manager was frustrated with his subordinates' constant negative reports. They regularly bemoaned the problems facing the organization, until one day the executive decided to put a stop to it. He instructed his staff never again to bring the term "problem" into the staff meeting. Instead, they were only to bring "opportunities" with them for discussion and resolution.

This worked well until the day a flustered young manager entered their staff meeting an hour late. His shirt was torn, there was grease on his face, and sweat poured off his brow. His appearance and late arrival shocked those in attendance into a stunned silence. Finally the top executive asked the question on everyone's mind: "What happened to you?!" Mindful of the mandate never to mention the word *problem*

> I JUST FOUND AN "OPPORTUNITY" THAT IS GOING TO PUT US OUT OF BUSINESS!

again, the frustrated young manager tried several times to recount his story, only to stop in midsentence. Red cheeks glowing with frustration, he finally blurted out, "Well, Boss, I just came across an 'opportunity' on the shop floor that I think is going to put us out of business!"

In reality, all organizational leaders must keep a watchful eye out for critical issues—which could either put them out of business or do severe damage to the organization. I like the term *critical issue* more than the term *problem* for one simple reason. Problems are often subtly hidden in what can often seem like insignificant events: a few customers complain about the quality of a product, attendance drops at church, fuel costs rise slightly, absenteeism rises for two months in a row. So, are these problems? Meaningless events? Random happenings? Initially, no one knows for sure. These situations should not be ignored, however. Any one of them could signal a change that could jeopardize the organization's success. Yet how can anyone keep track of all the potential problems that exist? The reality is that no one can. Nevertheless, when each member of the organization takes responsibility to watch for changes that occur in his or her area, then it is possible to minimize the negative impact of new critical issues.

This is accomplished by identifying success measures, such as profitability, quality, productivity, employee satisfaction, and so on, and then tracking their progress on a regular basis. When (not if) a critical issue is identified, then an appropriate strategy is crafted to minimize its negative impact on the organization.

Competitive Opportunities: Unexpected Doors to Success

Unlike critical issues, competitive opportunities are those wonderful instances when conditions actually change for the better. For example, productivity goes up, attendance increases, rejects go down, and so on. These positive occurrences require as much scrutiny as their evil cousins, the critical issues. Why? Since they are unexpected, there is no plan for how to sustain the positive change or to repeat the process for future success. Watchful people must ask themselves the *why* question whenever something good happens unexpectedly. *Why* did quality increase? *Why* are people suddenly beginning to attend our church? *Why* are our profits increasing? Competitive opportunities often tiptoe in unannounced and, unless grasped, disappear moments later.

For watchful leaders the possibility of new competitive opportunities is very real. Tax breaks, improved labor/management relations, product innovation, and/or potential mergers may all unexpectedly contribute to the organization's success.

A Practical Example

Problems and opportunities may surface at any time, and usually do so when least expected. When they do occur, they must be addressed quickly and decisively. Here is an example of how this works in the world of industry.

At the start of a year, a manufacturing organization's leaders decide to expand their business (competitive opportunity). In response, planning is done, resources are allocated, and new markets are pursued. So far, so good. Midway through the year, however, the organization is faced with new government regulations that require a complete product redesign (critical issue). So now what?

The leaders must now add the product redesign project to their already-full plate and make some very tough decisions. Since budgets have already been established for the year and work assignments have been made, there may not be enough finances and/or personnel to make the changes without making cuts elsewhere. Now the leaders begin the painstaking process of determining which issue is the most critical for the organization's success. They do so by answering a few questions that focus on priorities, resources, and long-range plans. For example, is the product redesign project more important than some ongoing research and development? Is it more important than servicing existing clients with products that may be in the later stages of their viability? Is it more important than the planned business expansion? Once these questions are answered, the leaders use their best judgment in addressing the most vital issues and decide where to invest their precious resources.

The Need for Daily Vigilance

Failure to identify and address critical issues and competitive opportunities in a timely manner is disastrous for any organization. In the church world, for example, some ministry leaders ignore critical issues and fail to look for new opportunities to serve their communities. The result? Those pastors typically see their formerly faithful followers leave to worship elsewhere. Too many religious leaders stubbornly continue to do what they always have done, despite the fact that both the size of their congregations and their levels of influence steadily decline.

Sadly, these organizations often fall into the "program trap." By this I mean that they implement a variety of special initiatives hoping to drum up interest in their disintegrating organization. Visitation programs, fundraisers, and other special events take the place of solid services aimed at changing lives. These programs just don't work. A much better approach is to have church leaders honestly evaluate the condition of their organization and identify potential changes that have occurred. Then they need to adjust their sights to focus or refocus on their original vision and values. Finally, they need to make appropriate changes to see vitality come back into their work.

Long-Term Success

Long-term success is possible. In fact, it is probable if leaders maintain a watchful eye on any changes, good or bad, that impact their organization. Once the changes are identified, then some solid problem solving will eliminate the threat or help the organization capitalize upon the opportunity. Our next chapter shows how to get all the members of an organization successfully involved in the problem-solving process.

CHAPTER 26

Solving Problems . . . Together

As an organization matures, many of the old roadblocks to success are removed. People are no longer confused about what to do, because there is a clear mission to follow and goals to accomplish. Unnecessary internal conflicts have lessened and unity has increased. Open lines of communication replace mistrust and misunderstanding. It sounds perfect—and it is, except for the ongoing emergence of our friendly enemy: change.

No matter how clear the mission or how sound the values, an organization always runs into changes along the way. Something breaks; someone stops communicating; a new competitor shows up. When these occur, a swift and professional response is needed. In the old days, that meant that a few top people in the organization rolled up their sleeves and attempted to solve the problem. Today there is a better way: solving problems . . . together.

The Problem with Problems

We all wish that problem solving could be easier than what it is, since we face so many problems each and every day. Sometimes we fail to find a solution; at other times we solve one problem only to discover that our solution caused another problem to spring up.

I recall hearing about a wealthy gentleman living in a northern climate who experienced just that. It seems that he had grown tired of shoveling snow off his sidewalk each winter, so he planned to solve this problem permanently when he built a new house. His innovative solution was simple: when he constructed his majestic new home, he installed heating pipes under his concrete driveway and sidewalks. According to his design, the pipes would heat the cement during the winter to melt any snow that dared to fall on his domain.

When the first heavy snowfall came, he excitedly turned on his heating system and waited for the results. His system worked to perfection; his was the only sidewalk in the neighborhood to remain free of snow. The man went to sleep confident that his neighbors soon would flock to his property to marvel at his new invention. The next morning he awoke to find that he was half right in his prediction. He discovered that his neighbors' dogs found his snow-free sidewalks an ideal place to relieve themselves. Evidently the canines found the warm surface a welcome alternative to cold sidewalks or snow-covered grass. His four-legged neighbors liked this innovation so much that they came to show their appreciation daily. That winter the gentleman problem-solver had something other than snow to shovel!

Problem Solving and Long-Term Success

Every organization experiencing positive change also encounters many problems along the way. This is normal, natural, and can even be extremely constructive if the problems are resolved properly. The secret is to have all members of the organization ready, willing, and able to participate in problem solving on a daily basis.

Remember, the alternative creates gridlock when leaders try

to solve all problems and make all decisions regarding their organization. In these absurd settings employees sit and watch their leaders stumble around, vainly looking for answers that already reside within the minds of their subordinates. Leaders who play the role of resident expert in all things soon render themselves ineffective. Why? Because conditions change so rapidly that one leader cannot possibly keep up with them all.

Problems must be solved *as* they arise in order to keep the organization moving ahead. If that statement is true, then the only rational approach is to train people at all levels so that they understand their authority, boundaries, and what resources are available to them. Once they are trained, then empower them to attack problems immediately! An organization's effectiveness accelerates exponentially once its members have mastered problem solving and are authorized to use their skills within their own areas of responsibility.

Finding the Proper Balance

As we have seen, it makes little sense to have a few leaders attempt to address all organizational problems without any input from others. At the opposite end of the spectrum is an approach where every problem is assigned to a formal committee for resolution. As in all things, there is a proper balance point that must be discovered.

Leaders spend much of their time solving problems, making decisions, and formulating plans, as well they should. Many of the issues they face require their immediate individual attention, and it would be inappropriate to delegate them to subordinates. Some organizational situations, however, are ideally suited for team input. For instance, when problems affect more than one person or one area of operation, then a team may be more effective in finding solutions, as opposed to just one person acting alone. Another prime situation for broader input is when an organization is attempting to solve a systemic problem that crosses many lines of authority. In these instances, it is helpful for representatives from the different areas to come together to analyze the situation.

There's a lot of truth to the old saying "Two heads are better than one." The modern term for this concept is *synergy*, which means that one plus one is *greater than* two. From an organizational perspective, when two or more people jointly combine their insights about a problem, then the solution is likely to be better than if they had tried to analyze it separately. In some instances the solution may not necessarily be better; however, it will have been discovered more swiftly. As a final benefit of cooperative problem-solving efforts, the final solution will have more support during the implementation phase because of the joint effort.

Successful Problem Solving

A problem-solving session should be one of the most exciting parts of any workday. The potential is astronomical when two or more people gather together to share their knowledge, wisdom, and insights. This provides a great opportunity for the power of agreement to be released. I have personally seen trained groups of problem-solvers discover millions of dollars in cost savings, streamline work processes, and create new approaches to customer service. I need to underscore the fact that the people involved were trained. In reality, problem-solving efforts succeed *only* when the individuals involved are properly prepared.

This means that interpersonal relationships are solid and that no hidden agendas exist. It is also crucial that all members of the organization use a common approach and agreed-upon terms when attempting to solve problems. The basic logic and sequence of problem-solving steps can be learned quickly and used for a lifetime.

The Problem-Solving Process

Much of the problem-solving training material on the market in the mid-1980s was difficult for people to comprehend and apply in a short period. In addition, some terms used in the training added more confusion than clarity for the learners. In response, I designed the following seven-step problem-solving process that has been used by thousands of people since that time.

The goal of this approach is twofold. First, I wanted to teach all members of an organization to think rationally, logically, and sequentially when facing a problem. Second, I sought to empower people with a common approach and easy-to-understand terms to use in problem-solving sessions. Here are the steps in the process.

Step 1—Identify the Problems. The first step in problem solving is to identify each problem clearly by stating its impact, when it began, and if the cause of the problem is known or unknown.

Step 2—Prioritize the Problems. Once a list of problems has been compiled, the problems must be listed in order of priority. This can be a challenge when more than one person is involved, because of differences in the perception of each problem's importance. A simple method of ranking the problems is used to avoid endless discussions fueled by personal agendas.

Step 3—Identify Probable Causes. Here people collect the information necessary to discover what has caused the problem. Different methods are taught for general, process, and people problems.

Step 4—Confirm Actual Cause. In this step, various charts, graphs, statistical process control charts, flow diagrams, and other tools are used to confirm the actual cause or causes of the problem. Each person involved learns how to create each type of data collection tool and how to interpret them.

Step 5—Set Solution Goals. All too often, solutions are implemented that solve the original problem but create larger problems somewhere else in the organization. This can be avoided by setting specific goals for each solution. These goals are used to determine if a proposed solution is ideal, acceptable, or unacceptable.

Step 6—Decide on a Solution. Most problems have more than one solution. Therefore, each alternative needs to be analyzed to determine cost, return on investment, time to implement, and impact on other parts of the organization. Then the most appropriate solution is selected for implementation.

Step 7—Develop an Action Plan. Many proposed solutions fail because of poor planning before implementation. This final step of the problem-solving process teaches the importance of clear assignment of responsibilities, timelines, documentation, and follow-up to insure that the solution has actually eliminated the problem.

The Power of Problem-Solving Training

Problem-solving training should always help people develop a logical, systematic approach to problem analysis. Once this approach has been mastered, it can be applied to virtually any problem situation in that person's professional or personal life. In many instances the understanding of a systematic problem-solving process is just as valuable as having detailed knowledge about a particular product or work process.

In recent decades many companies have tried to implement programs aimed at improving product quality. These programs continue to be called by many different names, such as Statistical Process Control, Six Sigma, Quality Improvement Programs, and countless others. Some of these programs produce outstanding results; others fail miserably for some predictable reasons.

I recall one organization that sent all of its managers, supervisors, and production employees to a two-day training seminar on the topic of quality improvement. The training was introductory, at best, and certainly didn't prepare the workforce to be proficient in statistical methods. Failing to realize this, corporate management expected immediate results as soon as the training ended. They demanded that the poorly prepared employees begin to draw statistical process control charts for each machine in their sizable operation. Many of the employees couldn't remember how to plot the points correctly on the charts, or even why they were doing it in the first place. That was a bad sign . . .

During a visit to the company I was amazed to see that some employees had literally drawn points and lines off the charts and onto the wall that held the chart, without making any adjustments to correct the obvious quality problems. They forgot that management wanted quality *parts*, not quality *charts*! Management soon decided to expose their employees to a complete course in problem solving and strategic thinking. Once the employees understood the entire process, it was much easier for them to comprehend how the techniques of quality measurement worked.

Another client of ours was having a problem with customer complaints about contaminants in its products that were packaged in fifty-gallon drums and sent by rail to multiple destinations. Several of the company's most knowledgeable staff studied the situation and concluded that there were only two possible stages in the manufacturing and delivery process where contamination could occur.

> THE EMPLOYEES FORGOT THAT MANAGEMENT WANTED QUALITY PARTS, NOT QUALITY CHARTS!

The experts focused their entire problem-solving effort on these two stages. After weeks of study, they attempted to implement their two-part "solution." First, they lectured employees who handled the material on the importance of being "careful." This initiative produced no change in product quality and did nothing to eliminate the contamination. Next, the experts purchased new equipment to load and seal the drums, thinking that would clear up the problem. Unfortunately, this expensive undertaking didn't work and customers still complained about contaminants in the product. This frustrating pattern of trial and error continued for months.

During this same period a group of production employees was being trained in our problem-solving methods and decided to study the problem of the contaminants as part of the training course. When these novices completed a systematic process chart on the problem, they were amazed to discover that there were at least *eighteen* different stages in manufacturing and delivery where contaminants could potentially get into their product. The trainees' findings were shared with the "experts"; and within weeks the problem was solved—permanently.

Who Are the Experts?

I am a firm believer in the importance of highly trained and specialized individuals, or "experts." These people are like deep pools from which others can drink. However, I also am a firm believer in the notion that *every* person is an expert in his or her particular field, position, area, or job. Individual superstars rarely win championships—it takes every member of a team to bring about success. Innovation and invention frequently come from ordinary people with extraordinary insight. It is often better to be an expert problem-solver than to be an expert in just one subject, one product, or one system.

Successes like the problem-solving team's discovery described above can become commonplace in any organization. All it requires is the organizational leaders' willingness to invest in the training of its members and then to give them opportunities to use their skills. In this type of environment, problems are quickly addressed and resolved by the people closest to the situation.

Organizations that utilize their human resources this way soon experience a wonderful transition from problem solving to problem prevention and, finally, to capitalizing on competitive opportunities. In these dynamic environments, team members now use their formidable skills to anticipate problems, improve on existing processes, and develop new products and services.

This results in an organization that is able to adjust quickly to any new critical issue and to seize upon emergent competitive opportunities, even before the competition knows that they exist.

CHAPTER 27

CASE STUDY

Beyond Success

The Malachi Global Foundation

The Malachi Global Foundation was conceived in 1997 but did not take its first real breath until the fall of 2002. I have included it here as a case study for two reasons: first, to show that the power of agreement process has application in nonprofit corporations just as readily as it does in any other type of organization; second, and more importantly, to help leaders realize the need to add a greater dimension of personal significance to their organizational success. All too often, professional men and women work for a few decades and then set their sights upon retirement—rather than upon the next great adventure, reserved just for them.

I remain convinced that the lessons learned during organizational change management can be easily applied to some of this world's greatest challenges. All it takes is for someone with vision to try something new and then watch what happens. My invitation to my middle-aged and golden-aged friends is to forgo traditional retirement in favor of a nontypical "*refire*ment." So many challenges in our world will only be overcome by seasoned, mature men and women willing to remain engaged in the process. Golf and fishing can wait. Many find it infinitely more satisfying to identify a cause larger than themselves and then to pursue it passionately. Such was the case with the Malachi Global Foundation.

Passionate Pursuit

The Malachi Global Foundation is my baby. It was formed to help parents and their children connect on meaningful levels, thereby improving the quality of life for families all over the world. Some of my associates and I created the organization for one basic reason—we saw a need that touched our hearts and we wanted to get involved. It was that simple.

Here is how this new organization began. In the summer of 1997 I became deeply concerned about the plight of our world's young people and wondered why so many of them fell victim to substance abuse, violence, suicide, and other destructive activities. This subject became increasingly important to me as my own children reached their teen years. After speaking with many people throughout the world and reading countless books on youth culture, I concluded that there were three missing ingredients from our approach to child rearing. They are lifelong mentoring, intentional blessing, and modern-day rites of passage.

Armed with this belief, I put together a pilot program for my own oldest son, Christopher. The culmination of that program was a rite of passage, or celebration, held for him when he turned thirteen. Thirty men attended that first event, bringing with them letters and symbolic gifts for my son. The celebration was extremely powerful and served to launch Christopher into his destiny as a mature young man.

Following the rite of passage, many of the attendees asked for an outline of the evening so that they could host similar rites of passage for their own sons and daughters. Rather than just writing an outline, I decided to write a book, entitled *Boy's Passage – Man's Journey,* to serve as a guide for others to follow. The book's release stirred many adults into action, and soon celebrations were being held across the country and then in different nations of the world. As a result, people began to send letters and e-mails asking for additional information on the subject. Many single mothers and grandparents asked for suggestions on how they could help young people with mentoring, blessing, and rites of passage.

Getting Started

As with all organizations, the Malachi Global Foundation began with a number of people who shared the same vision. Our initial team of leaders included my wife, Kathleen, Ric Olson, Scott Moore, Harry Marcus, Ron Williams, Jim Weidmann, and many others. We used a biblical passage, Malachi 4:6, as the catalyst for the MGF vision. This passage describes a wonderful situation where the hearts of fathers turn to their children and, as a result, the hearts of children turn to their fathers. With so much division in homes today, this seemed like a great vision to pursue. Using this as our cornerstone, we then followed the pattern described in this book, beginning with the creation of a mission statement:

The Malachi Global Foundation exists to inspire and equip men and other mentors with the tools needed to successfully reach, raise, love, and disciple the next generation.

Once the mission was set, we identified the basic needs of the organization. They were personnel, training manuals, teaching CDs, marketing strategies, mass media outlets for our message, a professional website, and locations at which to host retreats, conferences, and seminars. Next, we established primary goals and converted the goals into various projects. Once the projects were identified, we assigned each one to a member of the team, who then took responsibility for its accomplishment. Naturally, we spent time discussing and agreeing upon our core values, operating principles, and timelines.

The Results

The results of our labors took several years to see, but they were worth the wait. Now the Malachi Global Foundation works with organizations throughout the world to host retreats for men, fathers and sons, and youth. Each attendee leaves the retreat with a specific written plan for reaching the children in his life, whether they are his biological, adopted, or foster children, his grandchildren, other relatives, or children who have no one else to look out for them.

We also have produced numerous books, tapes, and CDs that promote the message of the organization and teach families how to work together effectively. The book *Boy's Passage – Man's Journey* and its counterpart for daughters, *Girl's Passage – Father's Duty,* are used not only to teach adults how to connect with the next generation, but also as textbooks for study groups and personal development as well. Another interesting development is a television program that carries our message throughout the world. The program was offered free of charge after the president of a network was exposed to the message of Malachi Global Foundation.

The Malachi Global Foundation also uses numerous locations throughout the world for weeklong outdoor adventure retreats for fathers and sons. Some of the locations feature fly-fishing, horseback riding, hiking, and overnight campouts in the mountains. MGF employs the technology of the day, which permits easy registration and information dissemination on our website (www. malachiglobal.org). It has been extremely rewarding for those on our leadership team to read the comments and testimonies that are regularly sent to the website. It is always motivating to know that others have embraced the vision.

Now It Is Your Turn

I encourage successful people to seek opportunities to create new organizations and/or involve themselves in initiatives that meet special needs. It is not difficult to do. A few simple questions can lead to an entirely new career for anyone willing to ask them. For example, what situations in the world make you angry or sad? World hunger? Injustice? Disenfranchised youth? How about poverty? Perhaps the plight of neglected senior citizens? Another key question is this: What are your unique talents or abilities? Countless nonprofit organizations lack professionalism, leadership, and other resources. The addition of just one professional—like you—can mean the difference between failure and success. Win/win/win.

There is no shortage of challenges, needs, or opportunities around us. Many of them are just waiting for someone to step up and try to make a difference. This takes courage and determination. If it was easy, someone else likely would have done it by now. Please don't let that stop you. The rocking chair can wait. We have all had some level of success to get this far. Now let's add to our success a new level of significance, by getting involved. What a great way to "refire."

CHAPTER 28

The Journey Never Ends

One New Year's Eve I noticed an intriguing trend in the advertisements on television. Strangely absent was the endless stream of ads for the necessities of life, such as biscuits, breath mints, and toilet bowl cleaners. In their place was a blitz of commercials designed to capture the attention of the thousands of people making resolutions for change in the coming year. The ads promoted weight loss pills, exercise equipment, vitamins, discount fitness centers, and no less than three different products to help people stop smoking. Sponsors knew that these announcements on New Year's Eve would generate millions of dollars from an army of people wanting to change their lifestyles.

I am certain that some individuals seized the moment to become smoke-free, fat-free, and cholesterol-free for the rest of their lives. More power to them. Sadly, I am just as certain that the majority tried to make a change for the better and then fell back into their old ways. Interestingly, it seems that the advertisers held a similar conviction. In less than a month, the commercials once again featured candy bars and reclining lounge chairs. Why did they change? Because the sponsors knew that by February most resolutions were only vague memories and people were ready to return to their unhealthy routines.

Too often we set goals for positive change when we are inspired or under pressure, only to forget about them when the pressure is off. This is true for individuals and for organizations as well. There is a temptation to back off on some of the commitments made once the initial crisis or motivation wanes. This can happen so subtly. In business, perhaps one leader begins to mistreat followers or employees let their quality standards slide. Leaders in government may be enticed to squander time, money, and other resources on projects other than those that support their stated missions. In the home, parents who have made commitments to spend more quality time with their children are tempted to work just a few more hours each week. We have come too far to allow that to happen.

Success Is in Your Reach—Don't Stop!

In recent years we have learned that when a person performs a behavior for approximately twenty-eight days in a row, it becomes a habit. This should encourage anyone who has struggled to stay on a new diet or to quit smoking. It is also good news for people involved in organizational change. The principle is the same, although it may take considerably longer than twenty-eight days to transform a nation, business, church, or family. The truth remains, though, that when something is done consistently over a period of time, it becomes ingrained. What begins as a novelty soon becomes a habit, and ultimately transcends into a new way of life.

Success belongs to those who passionately and tirelessly pursue a vision, not to those who quit before the finish line is reached. Don't ever quit. Former First Lady Eleanor Roosevelt summed it up this way: "The future belongs to those who believe in the beauty of their dreams."

So follow your dreams for positive change; and regardless of how many challenges you face, never give in to that word *stop*. Instead, remember your vision, live by your values, and *go* forward!